1726

THE YEAR THAT DEFINED AMERICA

Eddie L. Hyatt

HYATT PRESS   *   2019

Grapevine, Texas 76051

Publish, and set up a standard;
publish and conceal not (Jeremiah 50:2).

1726: The Year That Defined America
By Eddie L. Hyatt

© 2019 by Hyatt International Ministries, Incorporated
ALL RIGHTS RESERVED.

Published by Hyatt Press
A Subsidiary of Hyatt Int'l Ministries, Incorporated

Mailing Address (2019)
Hyatt Int'l Ministries
P. O. Box 3877
Grapevine, TX 76099-3877

Internet Addresses
Email: dreddiehyatt@gmail.com
Web Site: www.eddiehyatt.com
Social Media: Eddie L. Hyatt

Unless otherwise indicated, all Scripture quotations
are taken from the New Kings James Version of the Bible.
© 1979, 1980, 1982 by Thomas Nelson, Inc. Publishers.

All pictures are in the public domain and were taken from
the Internet.

Cover and Book Design by Susan Stubbs Hyatt

ISBN: 978-1-888435-40-5

Contents

Preface

The vision for this book unfolded quite suddenly and rather unexpectedly during this past summer (2019). I sensed a stirring in my heart to reprint *America's Revival Heritage*, a book I had published in 2012. This edition would include a new chapter on how the Great Awakening (1726-1740) impacted slavery in America and, in fact, marked the beginning of its demise in America.

The original edition of *America's Revival Heritage* was the first book that I wrote as a result of a seven-hour encounter that I experienced with the Lord in 2010. In this amazing visitation, God restored my hope for America, and I saw, for the first time, that the Great Awakening had a direct bearing on the founding of our nation.

In response to this recent directive to reprint *America's Revival Heritage*, I began reading through the book, making notes where edits should be made based on my ongoing research. I also began work on the new chapter that I wanted to add about slavery. And as I researched and wrote about this topic, I was deeply stirred.

In my 2010 encounter with the Lord, I had become aware of the direct bearing of the Great Awakening on the founding of the nation. Now, in this 2019 encounter, I was seeing that the Awakening also had a direct bearing on the ending of slavery in America.

As I was working enthusiastically on this new edition, I happened to come across a project undertaken by the *New York Times* called *The 1619 Project*. This project is designed to commemorate the occasion of the first African slaves being brought to Colonial America 400 years ago in 1619. To my surprise, they insisted that 1619, rather than 1776, marked the founding of America. In their thinking, America was defined by what happened in 1619. My response was, "No! America was not defined by 1619. America was defined by 1726."

1726, of course, was the year the Great Awakening began. Slavery would never have been abolished had it not been for the Spiritual awakening that began that year and eventually transformed Colonial America.

As I continued researching and editing the original manuscript, it dawned on me that I was actually writing a new book. This was not the second edition of *America's Revival Heritage;* it was, in fact, a new book that I would call **1726**.

It is my desire that God will use this book to awaken many to our true American heritage and that it will be a spark igniting another Great Awakening across our land.

To contact Dr. Hyatt or to order any of his
resources, visit www.eddiehyatt.com.
His books are also available at
amazon.com.
To contact him about presenting
THE 1726 PROJECT
in your church, community,
Christian school or Bible school,
send an email to
DrEddieHyatt@gmail.com.

Chapter 1

The Redefining of America

> To destroy a people, you must first sever their roots.
>
> *Alexander Solzhenitzsyn*

For the first 150 years of America's existence, no one questioned the axiom *America is a Christian nation*. This did not mean that everyone was a Christian or that the nation officially sanctioned any denomination or religious sect. It meant, instead, that the nation's laws and institutions were founded on Christian principles and values. This fact was stated by the U. S. Supreme Court in 1892 in the case of Church of the Holy Trinity *vs* The United States.[1] After examining thousands of historical documents, the nation's highest Court declared,

> There is no dissonance in these declarations. There is a universal language pervading them all, having one meaning. They affirm and reaffirm that this is a religious nation . . .. From the discovery of this continent to the present hour, there is a single voice making this affirmation. These, and many other matters

---

[1] https://supreme.justia.com/cases/federal/us/143/457/

which might be noticed, add a volume of unofficial declarations to the mass of organic utterances that this is a Christian nation.

This truth concerning America's overt Christian history was acknowledged in a December 1982 article in *Newsweek* entitled "How the Bible Made America." It contained this insightful statement:

> For centuries [the Bible] has exerted an unrivaled influence on American culture, politics and social life. Now historians are discovering that the Bible, perhaps even more than the Constitution, is our founding document: the source of the powerful myth of the United States as a special, sacred nation, a people called by God to establish a model of society, a beacon to the world.[2]

This reality of America being a Christian nation was expressed in American culture by Bible reading and prayer being common occurrences in all kinds of public settings. Until the 1960s, it was common for school days, school activities, sporting events, city council meetings, and other public events to open with prayer. Displays of Bible verses, crosses, and the Ten Commandments were common in public buildings, including courtrooms. It was normal for a baccalaureate sermon by a local pastor to be part of public school graduation exercises.

The Attack on Public Displays of Faith

---

[2] Kenneth L. Woodward with David Gates, "How the Bible Made America," *Newsweek*, 27 December 1982, 44.

The nation was shocked, therefore, when, in two Supreme Court rulings, Engel *vs* Vitale (1962)[3] and Abington School *vs* Schempp (1963),[4] the nation's highest court banned school-sponsored prayer and Bible reading in the public schools of America. This ruling was based on a contorted and novel interpretation of that part of the First Amendment that reads, "Congress shall make no law concerning the establishment of religion, or hindering the free exercise thereof."

This ruling opened the floodgates of anti-Christian activism. Since that time, lawsuits filed by atheist and secularist organizations have resulted in the removal of crosses, Ten Commandment displays, and other Christian expressions from public property. School children can no longer sing *Joy to the World* or *Hark! The Herald Angels Sing* at Christmas because of the Christian content. As part of this crusade to de-Christianize America, the secularists insist on calling a Christmas Tree a *Holiday Tree* and referring to the Christmas Holiday as *The Winter Holiday*.

Veterans groups and military chaplains have been told they cannot pray in *the Name of Jesus.* A high school coach was told he can no longer kneel to pray at the end of football games, and a high school band in Mississippi was ordered by a judge to remove *How Great Thou Art* from the repertoire of music that they play at football games and other school events. On April 6, 2009, President Barak Obama announced to a Turkish audience, "America is not a Christian nation." His audacious statement showed the extent to which the crusade to de-Christianize America had arrived.

---

[3] https://www.uscourts.gov/educational-resources/educational-activities/facts-and-case-summary-engel-v-vitale

[4] https://www.loc.gov/item/usrep374203/

The Attack
on America's Christian Heritage

In addition to the attack on Christian speech and symbols, there has been a purposeful revising of America's history, eliminating the stories of faith that permeate the nation's founding. For example, it is now normal for students to be taught that the Pilgrims came to America for monetary gain and that the Founders were people of the Enlightenment with little interest in God and matters of faith.

This attempt to redefine America by rewriting her history is a vital part of the secularist strategy to transform the America of Washington, Jefferson, Madison, and Lincoln. The fact is that peoples and nations derive their sense of identity from their history. To remove or revise a people's history is to make those people vulnerable to being easily molded into something different. Karl Marx was referring to this reality when he wrote, "People without a heritage are easily persuaded."[5]

In her book, *The Rewriting of America's History*, Catherine Millard documents just how pervasive this crusade to change America's history is. She points out that this is being carried out, not only in the rewriting of textbooks, but also in the rewriting of the original inscriptions on national monuments, changing the meaning to something other than the original intent. She writes,

> It is happening through the rewriting and/or reinterpretation of America's historical records: in our national parks, monuments, memorials,

---

[5] Cultural Legacy,
https://www.culturallegacy.org/resources/editorials/223128411.html

landmarks, shrines, and churches. In some cases, changes are subtle, and in others, blatant. It's done through removal of key historic pieces that do not support the current ungodly bias.[6]

The most recent attempt to redefine America by rewriting her past is the New York Times' *1619 PROJECT*. 1619 is the year that the first African slaves arrived in America. The stated goal of *The Times'* project is to "reframe" American history by claiming that 1619, not 1776, represents the country's true founding. They claim, therefore, that America is racist and corrupt at its very core and in need of fundamental change.[7]

Certainly, slavery is a blight on America's history. However, because of what happened in 1726, America is not defined by what happened in 1619. It was in 1726 that a great spiritual awakening began that shaped the spiritual and moral character of America's founding generation. It also broke down racial and cultural barriers, releasing anti-slavery sentiments that would eventually bring about the end of slavery in America. To understand America, one must understand the significance of what happened in 1726.

America Must Know about 1726

Recovering this truth about America's history is critical, for as George Orwell said in his classic book *1984*, "Whoever controls the past, controls the future." And commenting on

---

[6] Catherine Millard, *The Rewriting of America' History* (Camp Hill, PA: Harrison House, 1991), iii.

[7] https://www.nytimes.com/interactive/2019/08/14/magazine/1619-america-slavery.html

the demise of nations in world history, Carl Sandburg, winner of two Pulitzer Prizes, said,

> When a nation goes down, or a society perishes, one condition may always be found; they forgot where they came from. They lost sight of what had brought them along.[8]

Recovering the knowledge of what happened, beginning in 1726, is paramount, therefore, in getting it right about our nation. That year, a great spiritual *tsunami* began that eventually engulfed Colonial America in a flood of religious fervor. This *Great Awakening*, as it has been called, not only renewed the vision of the Pilgrims and gave birth to an anti-slavery movement, but also had a direct bearing on the founding of the United States of America. In fact, 1726 was the year that defined America.

---

[8] https://www.quotes.net/quote/37485

Chapter 2

America:
The Original Vision

Having undertaken for the glory of God,
and the Advancement of the Christian Faith ...
a Voyage to plant the first colony
in the northern parts of Virginia;
[we] Do by these Presents, solemnly and mutually
in the Presence of God and one another,
covenant and combine ourselves together into a civil Body
Politick for our better Ordering and Preservation,
and Furtherance of the ends aforesaid.

The Mayflower Compact, 1620

What happened in 1726 was not completely foreign to the populace at that time, for religious awakenings have been a part of the American experience from the nation's inception. Many of the first pilgrims to this land were Christian revivalists and reformists. Dissatisfied with the state of Christianity in their native lands, they came to America hoping to forge a more vital and Biblical form of Christianity. It would seem that spiritual awakening is in our national DNA.

The Pilgrims, who landed in Plymouth, Massachusetts in 1620, for example, were Separatist Puritans who were seeking, not only to reform the existing churches of Europe, but also to form a new church and social order based on the New Testament. In contrast to the cold, formalized orthodoxy of the state churches of Europe, they took the New Testament as their guide and preached a personal, living faith that could be known, not only "in the head," but also experienced "in the heart."

Puritans
Seek Reformation in England

Puritanism originally arose as a reform movement within the Church of England through people who felt that the English Church had retained too much of the old Roman Catholic order and was in need of further reform. The English Reformation had begun in the 1530s, based largely on personal and political motives. Henry VIII (1491–1547) had requested an annulment of his marriage to Catherine of Aragon (1485–1536) because she had failed to bear him a male heir to his throne. Henry's plan was to obtain an annulment and marry Anne Boleyn (1501–1536). When the pope and the Roman Catholic Church refused his request, he severed ties with Rome and was able to have the English monarch — in this case, himself — made the Head of the English Church. He was then able to proceed with his marriage to Anne Boleyn.

Because Henry had little interest in doctrinal and ecclesiastical reform, the Church of England differed little from the medieval Roman Catholic Church. But when Henry died in 1547 and was succeeded by the youthful Edward VI (1537–1553), the work of reform greatly accelerated, because Edward was favorable to the Protestant cause.

Edward, however, died in 1553 and was succeeded by his sister, Mary of Tudor (1516–1558), who was committed to the Roman Catholic Church. Under her reign (1553-1558), 288 Protestants were burned at the stake for their Protestant convictions and many others fled the country and lived in exile. (Protestants also persecuted Catholics when they held the reins of power.) When Mary died in 1558, she was succeeded by her sister, Elizabeth I (1533–1603), who was more favorable to the Protestant cause, and the work of reformation was renewed in the Church of England, also known as the Anglican Church.

Puritanism arose around 1560, during the reign of Elizabeth I, as a sort of *avant-garde,* leading the way in the English Reformation. "Puritan" was not a name they chose, since they simply thought of themselves as Christians. The name was put on them as an insult and slur by their critics. William Bradford, Governor of Plymouth said,

> And to cast contempt more upon the sincere servants of God, they opprobriously and most injuriously gave unto them the name of Puritans.[9]

The goal of Puritanism was to see the Church of England purged of all non-Biblical forms of worship and doctrine and renewed according to Scripture. The movement eventually separated, going in two different directions. One side believed that the Church of England could be reformed and so they continued to work within the institutional

---

[9] William Bradford, *Of Plymouth Plantation 1620-1647*, ed., Samuel Eliot Morrison (New York: Alfred A. Knoph, 2011), 9.

church. The other side believed that the state church was too corrupt and resistant to be reformed and so they formed "Separatist" congregations, which they sought to order according to the New Testament.

Separatist Puritans

The Separatists insisted that there was only one Head of the Church, and that it was not the British monarch. It was Jesus Christ. Since the Church of England was the official church of the nation, the Separatist congregations were considered illegal and a threat to the peace and stability of the nation. For this reason, they were severely persecuted by both civil and religious authorities.[10]

When Elizabeth I died in 1603 leaving no heir to the throne, she was succeeded by James VI of the Stuart Family of Scotland. He was crowned James I of England (1566–1625) and is best known, perhaps, as the King James of the Authorized King James Version of the Bible (1611).

James was not friendly toward the Puritan cause, and he was a staunch advocate of the Divine Right of Kings, a belief system in which the monarch was seen as God's representative in the earth, wielding absolute power over his subjects. To James, many of the doctrines and practices of the Separatists posed a serious threat to the state church and to his authority.

---

[10] Although illegal and severely persecuted, these Separatist and Nonconformist congregations began to gain prominence by the mid-1600s. The Act of Toleration of 1687 brought some relief, but they continued to be despised and treated with disdain by the government and much of society. John Wesley's grandfather on his mother's side, Dr. Samuel Annesley (1620-1696), was a separatist minister who was known as the "St. Paul of the nonconformists."

Consequently, he ordered, "Conform yourselves or I will harry you out of the land."[11]

> The Separatists were hounded, bullied, forced to pay assessments to the Church of England, clapped into prison on trumped-up charges, and driven underground. They met in private homes, to which they came at staggered intervals and by different routes, because they were constantly being spied upon.[12]

Puritans and the King James Bible

James, in particular, did not like the Geneva Bible (1560), the translation used by the Puritans. This translation had been produced by Puritans who had fled the tyrannical reign of Mary of Tudor and who had found refuge in John Calvin's city-state of Geneva. While there, they produced this new English translation, which included explanatory notes.

When Elizabeth I replaced Mary Tudor on the English throne in 1558, many Puritans began returning to their homeland, bringing with them the Geneva Bible. In 1560, they began publishing it in England and it soon became the most popular version of the Bible in England, especially among the Puritans.

It wasn't the translation that irritated James so much as those pesky notes in the margins. For example, in Acts 5:29 where Peter told the Jewish authorities, *We ought to obey God*

---

[11] Benjamin Hart, *Faith and Freedom: The Christian Roots of American Liberty* (Dallas: Lewis & Stanley, 1988), 69.

[12] Peter Marshall and David Manuel, *The Light and the Glory* (Grand Rapids: Fleming H. Revell, 1977), 108.

rather than man, the commentators of the Geneva Bible explained to their readers that they were obligated to obey monarchs and church leaders only so far as such obedience was also obedience to God. Also, a marginal note for Exodus 1:9 indicated that the Hebrew midwives were correct in disobeying the Egyptian king's orders. These and other similar comments were enough to raise the ire of kings, popes, and bishops who were used to having it their way, period.

King James, understandably, saw the Geneva Bible as a threat. In fact, he considered the marginal notes in the Geneva Bible to be "a political threat to his kingdom." This prompted the late Dr. D. James Kennedy, in his excellent book, *What if America Were a Christian Nation Again?* to write,

> His push for that 1611 translation was essentially an anti-Puritan measure. King James I set out to translate the Scriptures in order to replace an influential version he disdained, the Geneva Bible, which came out in 1560 and was widespread for two generations. The Pilgrims and Puritans loved this Bible. It was the footnotes . . . on the sides and at the bottom. Commentaries on passages such as "We ought to obey God rather than men" (Acts 5:29) that were enough to raise any monarch's eyebrows."[13]

James, therefore, commissioned the production of a new *authorized* translation without notes. We know this translation today as the King James Version or the Authorized King James Bible. Although this KJV eventually became the most popular translation in the English world, it was the Geneva

---

[13] D. James Kennedy, *What if America Were a Christian Nation Again?* (Nashville: Thomas Nelson, 2003), 23.

Bible that the Pilgrims and early Puritans brought with them to America.

Finding a New Home

In 1606, one of the earliest Separatist congregations was formed in Scrooby, Nottinghamshire, with John Robinson as its pastor. Because of their precarious situation, they committed themselves to one another in a written covenant. In it, they promised to be faithful to God and to one another, no matter what persecution they might be called upon to endure. Persecution did come, and King James gave them the option of going to prison or of leaving the country. Choosing the latter, the entire congregation migrated to Holland in 1608.

In Holland, however, they were treated as second-class citizens. They were permitted to engage only in menial labor and were paid wages so low they could barely survive. Despite making every effort to face life cheerfully and courageously, the terrible conditions caused many to age quickly and even to die young.

They were also greatly distressed to see their children being led away from the faith and into immoral lifestyles by the influence of the prevailing culture. So, after twelve years, they decided to find a home where they could worship freely and live the Christian lifestyle that burned in their hearts and which, they believed, was according to Scripture.

They Find a New Home in America

They agreed that some members of the congregation would go ahead to the New World and that Pastor Robinson and the remaining members would follow later. They negotiated an agreement with a group of English businessmen, called "The Adventurers" by William Bradford (1590-1657), to fund their journey. The "Pilgrims," as they became known, agreed to reimburse them with interest from money they would make in the New World through farming, fishing, and fur trading.

With these important matters settled, the Pilgrims, set aside "a day of solemn humiliation" to seek the Lord's blessing and guidance before their departure on July 22, 1620. They began the day with Robinson exhorting them from Ezra 8:21, which reads, *And there by the river I proclaimed a fast that we might humble ourselves before our God* and *seek of him a right way for us.* . ... After Robinson's exhortation, Bradford says, "The rest of the time was spent in pouring our prayers to the Lord with great fervency, mixed with abundance of tears."[14]

The next day the entire congregation boarded the ship *Speedwell* to say their final goodbyes. When the word came that it was time to sail, Bradford said,

> Their reverend pastor falling down on his knees (and they all with him) with watery cheeks commended them with most fervent prayers to the Lord and his blessing. And then with mutual embraces and many tears they took their leaves one of another, which proved to be the last leave to many of them.[15]

---

[14] William Bradford, *Of Plymouth Plantation 1620-1647*, ed. Samuel Eliot Morrison (New York: Alfred A. Knoph, 2011), 47.

[15] Bradford, 48.

They sailed from Delfshaven, Holland, to Southampton, England, where they transferred to a ship called *The Mayflower*. After several delays, they set sail for America on September 6, 1620. In all, 102 passengers and 25 or 30 crew members made the journey. Included in the number were several "strangers" who had been recruited by the businessmen who funded the journey. These individuals, whose motives were purely monetary, proved to be a "thorn in the side" of the Pilgrims.

The Pilgrims intended to settle in the northern part of Virginia, but winds blew them off course, and in early November, they landed further north on the shores of Cape Cod. When some of the "strangers" began to complain and talk of mutiny, the Pilgrims took the situation in hand and drew up a written compact patterned after the church covenants that had become popular, especially among the Puritans in England.

The concept of *covenant* had become an important part of Puritan thinking concerning God's dealings with humanity. A covenant is an agreement containing promises and obligations for both parties who enter into covenant. The Puritans pointed out, for example, that God promised to bless Abraham as an individual and Israel as a nation if they would be faithful to Him and to the covenant that He made with them (Genesis 12:1-3,15:18-21; Deuteronomy 28). They also emphasized the New Covenant inaugurated by Jesus Christ, calling out a people unto Himself (Matthew 26:27; I Peter 2:9-10). This was the basis on which members of the congregation had signed a church covenant before moving from England to Holland about 12 years prior to their move to The New World.

Although church covenants were not uncommon among the Puritans, this was probably the first time a civil covenant had been inaugurated between a people and God. According to the late Harvard professor, Perry Miller, "The Separatists aboard the Mayflower found a covenant the obvious answer to the first problem of political organization."[16]

Known as *The Mayflower Compact*, this covenant reads, in part:

> In the name of God, Amen! Having undertaken for the glory of God, and the Advancement of the Christian Faith, and the Honour of our King and Country, a Voyage to plant the first colony in the northern parts of Virginia; [we] Do by these Presents, solemnly and mutually in the Presence of God and one another, covenant and combine ourselves together into a civil Body Politick for our better Ordering and Preservation, and Furtherance of the ends aforesaid.

It is interesting to note that, first and foremost, they gave two reasons for coming to the New World: the first, for the glory of God; and the second, for the advancement of the Christian faith. This completely undermines the secularist notion, commonly taught in American schools and colleges, that the Pilgrims' motives in coming to America were monetary.

Indeed, William Bradford (1590-1657), the long-time Governor of Plymouth, made clear the missionary motive in their coming to America. In his memoirs, he listed the various reasons they had for coming to America, including fleeing persecution in England and being treated as second-class

---

[16] Perry Miller, *Errand Into the Wilderness* (Cambridge, MA: Harvard Univ. Press, 1956), 38.

citizens in Holland. He then wrote,

> Lastly (and which was not least), a great hope and inward zeal they had of laying some good foundation, or at least to make some way thereunto, for the propagating and advancing of the gospel of the kingdom of Christ in those remote parts of the world; yea though they should be but even as stepping-stones unto others for the performing of so great a work.[17]

After signing *The Mayflower Compact* on November 21, 1620, the passengers disembarked, stepping onto the sands of Cape Cod near present day Provincetown. Bradford described their actions as they stepped ashore in the New World.

> Being thus arrived in a good harbor and brought safe to land, they fell upon their knees and blessed the God of heaven, who had brought them over the vast and furious ocean and delivered them from all the perils and miseries thereof. They had begun their long journey by kneeling on the dock at Delfshaven to ask God's blessing; they ended it on the sands of Cape Cod, kneeling to thank Him for that blessing.[18]

They moved across the bay from Cape Cod to a location that they called Plymouth, and there they established the first English settlement in New England. During that first, brutal winter, not having adequate food and shelter, the little group suffered. In fact, almost half of the congregation died of scurvy and other diseases brought on by the long, arduous voyage coupled with the austere conditions of their new surroundings.

---

[17] William Bradford, *Of Plymouth Plantation 1620-1647*, ed. Samuel Eliot Morrison (New York: Alfred A. Knoph, 2011), 25.

[18] Peter Marshall and David Manuel, 120.

Fortunately, about the time of the spring thaw, two Native Americans who spoke English befriended them. The Pilgrims believed that God sent them providentially to help them in their time of dire need. These two men, particularly *Squanto* of the Patuxet tribe, taught the Pilgrims how to farm, hunt, and fish. His instructions probably saved their lives, because in England, they had been craftsmen and townspeople, and without knowledge of these indispensable skills, they would not have survived in the wilderness of New England. But survive they did! And through hard work and God's providential care, they went on to flourish and to help lay the foundations for a great, new nation.

Their Failed Experiment with Socialism

The Adventurers—those who had funded the Pilgrims' journey to America—required that they live communally for seven years with everyone receiving the same compensation for their work. This meant that there was no private ownership; instead, everyone worked fields owned by the plantation. The harvest went into a common fund from which each family received a portion for their sustenance. The remaining balance was used to pay their debt.

The same was true of proceeds from fishing and fur trading. No one was rewarded for their individual labor. Everyone received an equal amount for their basic necessities, and the rest went into the common fund. The agreement stated that at the end of seven years, assuming all debts were cleared, anything left in the common fund would be divided among the Pilgrim families.

Bradford, who served as Governor of Plymouth for over thirty years, told of the challenges of this socialist system. Young men, he said, tended to resent getting paid the same as older men who did less work than they did. As a result, many gave only a half-hearted effort, since they knew they would receive the same reward, no matter how hard they worked.

The older men, for their part, felt they deserved more honor and compensation because of their age, and they resented getting paid the same as the youngsters in their midst. Furthermore, Bradford said that the women often refused to go to the fields to work, complaining of headaches, and to have compelled them to go would have been considered tyranny and oppression.

So, this socialist system discouraged work and innovation, and it almost destroyed the colony. When it became obvious that lack and, perhaps, starvation would be their lot under this system, Bradford and the leaders of the colony decided to make changes. After much prayer and discussion, they decided to dispense with that part of the agreement that required them to live communally and to replace it with a free enterprise system.

They Experience the Gain of Free Enterprise

According to Bradford, they divided the land around them, allotting to each family a certain portion that would be theirs to work and use as they chose to meet their own needs. Bradford said that there was an immediate change. The young men began to work much harder because they knew they would enjoy the fruit of their own labors. There were no more complaints from the older men for the same reason. And now the women labored in the fields, taking the children with them, because they knew that they and their families would benefit personally.

Under this new system, instead of lacking food, each family now grew more food than they needed, and they began to trade with one another for furnishings, clothes, and other goods. They also had enough surplus to trade with the Native Americans for furs and other items. In short, the colony began to prosper when it dispensed with its socialist form of government and implemented, instead, a free, entrepreneurial system. Of their experience with socialism, Bradford wrote,

> This community [i.e., socialism] was found to breed much confusion and discontent and retard much employment that would have been to their benefit and comfort . . . and showed the vanity of that conceit of Plato's, and applauded by some of later times, that the taking away of property and bringing in community into a commonwealth would make them happy and flourishing; as if they were wiser than God.[19]

As a result of this failed experiment, going forward, Plymouth Colony practiced private ownership of property and free enterprise. Also, taking the Separatist form of church government as their model, they decentralized authority, and the people chose their leaders by election. They held annual elections for governor and for seven council members who assisted and advised the governor. They also had a written constitution by which they agreed to live, which we know as *The Mayflower Compact*. According to historian,

---

[19] Bradford, 120-21.

Benjamin Hart,

> What Abraham Lincoln described as government "of the people, by the people and for the people," was inherited from a tradition beginning with the Congregationalist Protestant settlement in Plymouth, Massachusetts, in the 1620s.[20]

---

[20] Benjamin Hart, *Faith & Freedom* (Dallas: Lewis and Stanley, 1988), 82.

Chapter 3

New England Covenants with God

We have entered into an explicit Covenant with God.
We have drawn up indentures with the Almighty, wherefore
if we succeed and do not let ourselves be diverted into
making money, He will reward us. Whereas if we fail,
if we fall to embrace this present world and prosecute
our carnal intentions, the Lord will surely break out
in wrath and make us know the price of the breach
of such a Covenant.

John Winthrop (1588 - 1649)
Founder of Boston, MA

Over the next few years, Separatists continued to migrate to Plymouth, but their numbers remained small until about 1630, when a new round of persecution was launched against all Puritans in England by Charles I (1600-1649). As a result, about twenty thousand Puritans immigrated to New England between 1630 and 1640.

Among the first to arrive in this new wave of immigration was a flotilla of seven ships carrying about seven hundred passengers. They were led by John Winthrop (1587/88–1649), a Cambridge scholar and former Justice of the Peace.

Winthrop had experienced a dramatic conversion to Christ and had aligned himself with the Puritan vision of a renewed and reformed Christianity in England and the world.

Entering into Covenant with God

During their journey across the North Atlantic, Winthrop composed a sermon entitled *A Model of Christian Charity*. In it, he exhorted his fellow travelers, saying that "the eyes of the world are upon us" and that God would have them, in their new home, be that "city on a hill" of which Jesus spoke in Matthew 5:14, a shining light, as it were, exhibiting a truly Biblical model of Christian living for the rest of humanity to see.

Like the Pilgrims who had preceded him, Winthrop considered their founding documents to be a covenant with God. He insisted that they had come to America, not to fulfill their own plan and purpose, but instead, to fulfill the plan and purpose of Almighty God. He spoke of the seriousness of this covenant with God into which they had entered, and he exhorted:

> We have entered into an explicit Covenant with God. We have drawn up indentures with the Almighty, wherefore if we succeed and do not let ourselves be diverted into making money, He will reward us. Whereas if we fail, if we embrace this present world and prosecute our carnal intentions, the Lord will

surely break out in wrath and make us know the price of the breach of such a Covenant.[21]

Drawing a parallel with Israel in the Old Testament, he insisted that, if they would walk uprightly before God and with one another, they would be greatly blessed in the land where they would make their new home. He said,

> We shall find that the God of Israel is among us, when ten of us shall be able to resist a thousand of our enemies; when He shall make us a praise and glory that men shall say of succeeding plantations, "may the Lord make it like that of New England." For we must consider that we shall be as a city upon a hill. The eyes of all people are upon us.[22]

Winthrop and his company assumed control of the Massachusetts Bay Company (1629) and brought its charter with them to America. They landed at what is now Salem, but later, they moved to the Shawmut Peninsula where they founded the city of Boston (1630) and the Massachusetts Bay Colony. Their pioneering efforts opened the way for the thousands of new immigrants who began to make their way to New England.

As a result of their clearly stated vision and the persecution in England carried out by Charles I and Archbishop William Laud (1573–1645), Puritans began pouring into the Massachusetts Bay Colony. Included in their numbers were

---

[21] Perry Miller, *Errand Into the Wilderness* (Cambridge, MA: Harvard Univ. Press, 1956), 5.

[22] John Winthrop, A Model of Christian Charity (1630), https://history.hanover.edu/texts/winthmod.html.

some of the best minds and most powerful preachers in England, leading Benjamin Hart to comment:

> Distinguished graduates from Cambridge and Oxford, "silenced" by Laud, poured into the colony, and many brought whole congregations with them. The houses of worship they built were bleak. There was no organ music, no stained-glass windows and no heating. The benches they sat on were hard. But nowhere in the world was the Gospel expounded more Masterfully from the pulpit.[23]

New England Covenants with God

With thousands of immigrants flooding into New England, new towns sprang up throughout Massachusetts, Connecticut, and Rhode Island. Virtually all new communities were founded on written documents patterned after the church covenants. These documents stated the reason for their existence, gave glory to God and prioritized the Gospel as their reason for being. For example, in the 1639 founding document of Connecticut, entitled *The Fundamental Orders of Connecticut,* is this statement:

> We, the inhabitants and residents of Windsor, Hartford, and Wethersfield, knowing where a people are gathered together the word of God requires that to maintain the peace and union of such a people there ought to be an orderly and decent government established according to God . . . we do for ourselves and our successors enter into combination and confederation together, to maintain and preserve the

---

[23] Hart, *Faith and Freedom,* 93.

liberty and purity of the Gospel of our Lord Jesus Christ, which we now profess.[24]

As the number of new towns increased, there arose a felt need for some sort of centralized government to facilitate mutual defense and to arbitrate land disputes. To meet this need, the United Colonies of New England was formed, and a constitution was formulated, patterned on the idea of covenant. Dated May 19, 1643, the opening statement of the constitution expressly states why they had all come to the New World. It reads,

> Whereas we all came into these parts of America with one and the same end and aim, namely to advance the kingdom of our Lord Jesus Christ and enjoy the Liberties of the Gospel in purity and peace.[25]

The constitution provided for each colony to have two representatives, forming a council of eight. This council was invested with power to arbitrate boundary disputes, coordinate mutual defense, and facilitate advice and mutual support. It clearly stated that this council existed for "preserving and propagating the truth and liberties of the Gospel."[26]

There is no question that this constitutional system, wherein each individual colony retained its autonomy, and the powers of government were limited by the constitution, was a forerunner of the federalist system that was created at Philadelphia in 1776 and 1787. The United Colonies of New

---

[24] Fundamental Orders of 1639, https://avalon.law.yale.edu/17th_century/order.asp

[25] William Bradford, *Of Plymouth Plantation 1620-1647*, Samuel Eliot Morison, ed. (New York: Alfred A. Knoff, 2011), 431.

[26] Bradford, *Of Plymouth Plantation 1620-1647*, 431.

England clearly foreshadowed the United States of America, both in its form of government and in its Christian character.

Clearly, the Puritans saw these written statements as covenants, not only among themselves, but also between their society and God. They believed that God dealt, not only with individuals, but also with social units, including families, churches and nations. According to Perry Miller, "The central conception in their thought is the elaborated doctrine of covenant."[27]

The Blessing and Responsibility of Covenant

These early immigrants saw Israel in the Old Testament as a model or pattern for their social covenant with God. Many, in fact, saw themselves as a new Israel. Like Israel of old, they believed that if they, as a people, would keep their part of the covenant, which was to walk uprightly and make His name known, they would be blessed. If, on the other hand, they were to lose their sense of divine purpose and live selfish and sinful lives, they believed that they would suffer God's wrath because of their failure to keep the covenant. During the voyage to New England, Winthrop warned,

> Now if the Lord shall please to bear us, and bring us in peace to the place we desire, then hath He verified this Covenant and sealed our commission . . . but if we fail to perform the terms of the Covenant, we shall perish out the land we are crossing the sea to possess.[28]

---

[27] Miller, 60.

[28] John Winthrop, *A Model of Christian Charity (1630)*, https://history.hanover.edu/texts/winthmod.html

This social responsibility to God is the reason the Puritans tended to hold one another accountable. They pointed out that, since communities and nations cannot be rewarded in the next world, they must necessarily be rewarded in this one, according to their deeds. They believed that the sin of one or a few could, therefore, bring down God's judgment on the entire community. This is also the reason that laws were passed outlawing adultery, fornication, profanity, drunkenness and Sabbath breaking.

These covenants meant that those who became a part of these communities were agreeing to be ruled, not by a monarch, but by laws upon which they all agreed. There is no question that these early covenants were precursors of the written statements that became the founding documents of the United States of America. As Gary Amos and Richard Gardiner say, "The early New England constitutions were covenants. These covenants clearly foreshadowed the United States Constitution."[29]

The Puritan Political Vision

The Puritan vision was for a state in which godly pastors exerted their influence, not only in the church, but also in the civic realm. Although church attendance was open to all, only those who could testify to a personal, saving relationship with Jesus Christ could be members. Only church members could vote in civic elections, and civic leaders were expected to be Christians who would consult with pastors concerning political and civic issues.

---

[29] Gary Amos and Richard Gardiner, *Never Before in History: America's Inspired Birth* (Richardson, TX: Foundation for Thought and Ethics, 1998), 43.

What the Puritans implemented in America was not a theocracy, but neither did they entertain any thought of a separation between church and state. They believed that God had created society as a unified whole to reflect His glory. Church and state, the individual and the public — these were all related spheres, and all were to function under the Lordship of Christ whose government was to be administered through pastors and godly civic leaders.

Interestingly, pastors were not allowed to hold political office in New England. This was based on the Puritans' belief that the corruption of the church had begun with the Roman Emperor Constantine (AD 306–337) when he began merging Christianity with the state and made the power of the state available to the bishops and priests. In their view, all churches and ministers that are pawns of the state inevitably become corrupt, and their goal was to maintain the purity of the faith in New England.

The Vision to Be That "City on a Hill"

Although persecuted in England, the Puritans came to America, not merely to escape the unpleasantries of their homeland, but also to pursue the reformation of Christianity, which they believed could be carried out more expeditiously in the New World. They believed that, in the wilderness of New England, they would demonstrate what could happen if a body of Christians were allowed to live their lives wholly unto God. Their vision was to become that "shining light" and "city on a hill" of which Jesus had spoken (Matthew 5:14).

According to Mark A. Noll, Professor of Church History at Wheaton College, the Puritan mission to America was "both to restore the purity of early Christianity and to be a "city on the hill" for those who remained in Europe."[30] Harvard professor, Perry Miller, described the great Puritan migration of 1630-40 as "An organized task force of Christians, executing a flank attack on the corruptions of Christendom." He went on to say,

> These Puritans did not flee to America; they went in order to work out the complete reformation which was not yet accomplished in England and Europe, but which they believed would quickly be accomplished back there if only the saints had a working model to guide them.[31]

The Puritan Emphasis on Education

Among those early Puritan immigrants to America, at least one hundred had received theological training at Cambridge. At least thirty others had received theological training at Oxford. It is, therefore, not surprising that, early on, there was a desire for an educational system that would prepare pastors for the churches and perpetuate the Puritan vision of Christian reform.

As a result, Harvard College, now Harvard University, was formed in 1636 to train ministers and pastors for the Puritan churches. Harvard was thoroughly Christian, and all students were to understand their education in the following terms:

> The main end of life and study is to know God and

---

[30] Mark A. Noll, *A History of Christianity in the United States and Canada* (Grand Rapids: Eerdmans, 1996), 47.

[31] Perry Miller, *An Errand Into the Wilderness* (Cambridge, MA: The President and Fellows of Harvard College, 1984), 11.

His Son Jesus Christ, which is eternal life, John 17:3, and therefore to lay Christ in the bottom, as the only foundation of all knowledge and learning. And seeing the Lord only giveth wisdom, let everyone seriously set himself by prayer in secret to seek it of him.[32]

In 1701, Puritans in Connecticut established Yale College, now Yale University, to give the youth a "liberal and religious education so that leaders for the churches should not be lacking."[33] In fact, all the early colleges in America were founded to train ministers and to propagate the rediscovered Christian message promoted by the Reformation. And these are the colleges in which the Founders of this nation received their training.

Lower levels of education were also important. In 1642, for example, the Massachusetts legislature threatened town leaders with fines if they did not see that all children were "trained to read and understand the principles of religion." Five years later, a law was passed requiring that each town of at least fifty households appoint a teacher for training the youth. Professor Noll points out that this attention to learning "made New England one of the world's most literate places by the end of the century."[34] Until after the Civil War, most educational programs in the United States from grade schools through universities were modeled on patterns established by the first Puritan settlers.[35]

---

[32] Shield and "Veritas" History,
http://www.hcs.harvard.edu/~gsascf/shield-and-veritas-history

[33] Earle E. Cairns, *Christianity through the Centuries* (Grand Rapids: Zondervan, 1981), 366.

[34] Noll, 44.

[35] Noll, 40.

Jamestown's Godly Vision

Although New England was the primary place where the writing of constitutions developed, all of the colonies were founded on similar social compacts with God. When the Jamestown settlers disembarked at Cape Henry, Virginia, on April 29, 1607, for example, their first act was to erect a seven-foot, oak cross that they had brought from England. They then gathered around the cross for a prayer service in which they dedicated the land that was to be their new home to God. In his dedicatory prayer, their chaplain, Rev. Robert Hunt (1569-1608), declared, "From these very shores the Gospel shall go forth to not only this New World but to the entire world."[36]

This act was in line with the official Virginia Charter, which recognized "the Providence of Almighty God" and expressed the desire that the establishment of the colony would "tend to the glory of His Divine Majesty." This document also expressly stated that the purpose of the colony was to propagate the "Christian religion to such people as yet live in darkness and miserable ignorance of the true knowledge and worship of God."[37]

There are amazing similarities among *The Virginia Charter,* *The Mayflower Compact,* and other founding documents of

---

[36] Richard Klein, "Faith of our Fathers: Spirituality in Jamestown," https://www1.cbn.com/churchandministry/faith-of-our-fathers%3A-spirituality-in-jamestown

[37] William J. Federer, *America's God and Country: Encyclopedia of Quotations* (St. Louis, MO: Amerisearch, 2013), 624.

New England. This led Harvard professor, Perry Miller, to suggest that Virginia and New England were not that different. He pointed out that both communities were children of the Reformation, "and what we consider distinctively Puritan was really the spirit of the times."[38]

Other Groups Looking for Revival and Reform

Other groups also came to America seeking freedom to express their faith. For example, the Dutch Reformed settled in New York and New Jersey, while Presbyterians from Scotland and Ireland settled in New York, New Jersey, and Maryland. One of the most persecuted groups in Europe, the Baptists, migrated mainly to Rhode Island, as well as to other regions throughout the colonies. Reform-minded Roman Catholics, committed to religious tolerance, settled in Maryland. The Quakers [i.e., The Religious Society of Friends] settled in Pennsylvania, a colony that became a haven for religious dissenters, because Quakers, along with the Baptists, were early champions of both freedom of conscience and the idea that the state should be neutral in its position regarding religion.

The Quakers and Pennsylvania

Pennsylvania flourished with almost no government from the time it was founded by William Penn (1644 – 1718) in 1681 until 1756, when the Quakers relinquished control, or *non-control*, of the colony. Quakerism had arisen as a radical revival/reform movement in England, especially between

---

[38] Miller, 105.

1650 and 1690. Taking reform a step beyond that of the Separatist Puritans, while retaining high regard for all people, the Quakers rejected all forms of government and outward ordinances for their churches. Instead of outward forms and regulations, they emphasized the inward work of the Holy Spirit, resident in each believer, which they called *the inner light* (John 1). They also emphasized the New Testament admonition of *brotherly love*.

Penn had received the territory from King Charles II as payment for a debt owed to his father . A devout Christian and Quaker, he applied the Quaker model of government, or *non-government*, to Pennsylvania. He drew up plans for the colony in 1682, and at the time, his naming its major city *Philadelphia*, spoke of how he envisioned it functioning. *Philadelphia* is derived from two words from the Greek New Testament: *phileo* meaning "love," and *adelphos* meaning "brother." So, *Philadelphia* means "City of Brotherly Love."

In his *Fundamental Constitution of Pennsylvania (1682), Penn* guaranteed freedom of worship for all, but in it, he laid out the following conditions of that freedom:

So long as every such person does not use this Christian liberty to licentiousness, that is to say, to speak loosely and profanely of God, Christ, or religion, or to commit any evil in their lifestyle.[39]

---

[39] Federer, 502.

Penn also authored *The Charter of Privilege of Pennsylvania* (October 2, 1701) in which he stated that only those who believed in Christ could hold public office. In the Charter, he says,

> ... all persons who profess to believe in Jesus Christ, the Savior of the world, shall be capable to serve this government in any capacity, both legislatively or executively.[40]

Because Penn expected the citizens of Pennsylvania to practice self-governance according to Christian principles, there were few outward laws and regulations. In fact, when the British official, John Blackwell, arrived in Philadelphia in 1688, he had difficulty locating the government offices. Finally, when he did locate them, he found them empty because the governing council met briefly only once or twice each year, as the need arose. To the surprise of many, in those early days and until 1756, both Pennsylvania and the City of Philadelphia flourished, with the population increasing 24-fold. During that same period, New York's population merely doubled.

The Quakers relinquished control of the colony as a result of several bloody Indian raids on remote settlements in the colony. Being pacifists, the Quakers were unwilling to take up arms to defend the settlers. Under pressure from influential citizens of Philadelphia, such as Benjamin Franklin (1706-1790), they finally gave up control of the colony in 1756.

Even so, the radical Pennsylvania experiment of religious and individual freedom had shown what can happen when

---

[40] Pennsylvania Charter of Privileges,
http://www.ushistory.org/documents/charter.htm 2

self-governed people are given the freedom to pursue their dreams under God. In his excellent book, *Faith & Freedom*, Benjamin Hart says,

> It would have been very difficult to explain exactly what it was that Americans were fighting for if the Quakers had not, in fact, implemented William Penn's political philosophy: especially, that government has no right to use force against individuals to serve the purposes of the community. There would have been no experience of such a society to point to without Pennsylvania. Quaker rule provided the needed historical precedent. They were averse to using force to an extreme. But it was the radical nature of the Quaker conception of government that led to the new political theory that would emerge between 1776 and 1787.[41]

The Quaker experiment reminds us that the freedoms enshrined in the American Constitution and Bill of Rights will only work when they are applied to a people who are self-governed by Christian principles of morality. Otherwise, freedom degenerates into anarchy and a means for the pursuit of selfish and ungodly ends. This is what John Adams (1735–1826) was referring to when he said, "Our Constitution was made only for a moral and religious people. It is wholly inadequate for the government of any other."[42]

---

[41] Hart, 205.

[42] From John Adams to Massachusetts Militia, 11 October 1798, https://founders.archives.gov/documents/Adams/99-02-02-3102

America's Christian Origins Are Undeniable

It is abundantly clear, then, that America was not settled by mild-mannered Christians who were tepid in their faith and reserved in their witness of that faith. These early immigrants were totally committed to Christ and were willing to make any sacrifice to advance the freedom that they believed was the God-given right of every human being. Hart expressed it well:

> It was Protestants of the most radical stripe, most zealous in their religious convictions (those whom the American Civil Liberties Union would like to see outlawed from the public discourse) who were in fact the greatest proponents of religious liberty as codified in America's governing charter 200 years later.[43]

Notwithstanding the religious squabbles that erupted at times among some groups, as well as the non-Christian behavior of others, there is no question that America's origins are rooted in a passion to recover and live out New Testament Christianity. In 1820, the noted United States Senator, Daniel Webster (1782–1852), speaking at the 200-year anniversary celebration of the landing of the Pilgrims at Plymouth, said,

> Finally, let us not forget the religious character of our origin. Our fathers were brought hither by their high veneration for the Christian religion. They journeyed by its light and labored in its hope. They sought to incorporate its principles with the elements of their society, and to diffuse its influence through all their

---

[43] Hart, 205.

institutions, civil, political, or literary. Let us cherish these sentiments and extend this influence still more widely; in the full conviction, that that is the happiest society which partakes in the highest degree of the mild peaceful spirit of Christianity.[44]

God Has No Grandchildren

A wise person once said, "God has no grandchildren." In other words, there is no automatic or formal passing of genuine faith from one generation to the next. Each generation must, in fact, know and experience God for itself. This truth was evident in the Puritan experience as the first generation passed from the scene and the children and grandchildren of the first Pilgrims began to establish themselves in the society which their parents had carved out for them in the New England wilderness.

[44] Marshall Foster and Mary-Elaine Swanson, *The American Covenant, The Untold Story* (USA: The Mayflower Institute, 1983), 158-59.

Chapter 4

The Vision Wanes

> The golden showers have been restrained;
> the influences of the Spirit suspended;
> the consequence has been that the gospel
> has not had any eminent success.
> Conversions have been rare and dubious;
> few sons and daughters have been born to God.
>
> *William Cooper (1693-1743)*

In spite of the hardships encountered in carving out a new life in the New World, the first generation of immigrants to America were normally vibrant in their faith and passionate in their vision for a revival of New Testament Christianity. Their children and grandchildren, however, while retaining many of the outward forms of worship and doctrine, tended to lose the vitality and vision of their parents and grandparents. As former generations passed from the scene, the original passion for Christian reform and renewal passed away with them, and succeeding generations were left *having a form of godliness but denying its power (II Timothy 3:5).*

Earthly Concerns Replace Spiritual Priorities

Nowhere was this more obvious than in New England, where, by the 1650s, the original Puritan vision for the complete reformation of Christendom had obviously subsided, being replaced by more worldly concerns. Whereas, through faith and a disciplined work ethic, the first generation of Puritans had created prosperity—not as a goal, but as the fruit of their lifestyle—the third generation of Puritan stock tended to make prosperity their goal. As the well-known Puritan pastor, Cotton Mather (1663-1728), put it, "Religion begat prosperity and the daughter devoured the mother."[45]

Even before his death in 1657, Bradford had lamented that the younger generation at Plymouth had lost the Spiritual passion and vision of their parents. [46] Commenting on Bradford's lament, Dr. Samuel Morris, editor of Bradford's work, wrote,

> In his later years the Governor felt that the glory had departed from Plymouth; the town declining in numbers, population dispersed, young people indifferent to religion and heedless of their fathers' sacrifices, luxury coming in with prosperity.[47]

The preoccupation with affluence and the acquisition of earthly goods also led to deteriorating relationships with the native people. Because the first generation of Puritans had been genuinely committed to reaching the native people with the Gospel, they had sought to build authentic, sincere friendships. Indeed, the Pilgrims and the first generation of

---

[45] Peter Marshall and David Manuel, 216.

[46] Bradford wrote, "O sacred bond, whilst inviolably preserved. How sweet and precious were the fruits that flowed from the same! But when this fidelity decayed, then their ruin approached. O that these ancient members had not died or been dissipated (if it had been the will of God) or else that this holy care and constant faithfulness had still lived, and remained with those that survived," 33.

[47] Bradford, xxvii.

Puritans treated the native people with what Dr. Samuel Eliot Morison called "a combination of justice, wisdom and mercy." They sincerely wanted to see the natives come to Christ and experience the joy of His salvation.[48]

But the lust for land by many in succeeding generations not only trumped their evangelistic zeal, but also led to a number of disingenuous treaties with several native tribes. Many of these tribes, already suspicious of the immigrants and their "new religion," were further alienated by these actions, and a number of bloody conflicts ensued. This further drained the spiritual life and vitality of the people.

Half-Way Christians

The loss of spiritual vitality among the Puritans was reflected in what they called *The Half-Way Covenant*. This was implemented in 1662 by second and third generation Puritans in an effort to stop the alarming loss of church members. It offered partial church membership to those who could not testify to a saving relationship with Jesus Christ, and it allowed these "nominal" Christians to have their children baptized without claiming full church membership. It was an indicator that many of the churches

---

[48] A prime example of this missionary vision is John Eliot (1604-1690) who translated the entire Bible into the native, Massachuset language, and it became the first Bible printed in America. His work spawned the establishment, in 1649, of the first missionary society, the Company for the Propagation of the Gospel in New England and Parts Adjacent in North America. These missionary endeavors, however, were often interpreted by the chiefs and medicine men as threats to their power, and they often looked upon the Puritans as intruders, both geographically and spiritually.

had deteriorated into formal religious institutions with no power to bring needed change.

Seventeen years later, in 1679, a group of ministers met in Massachusetts, and at the conclusion of their gathering, they issued a statement declaring: "God hath a controversy with His New England people." The members of this "Reforming Synod" formulated this statement because of the increase in ungodliness and spiritual indifference that they observed on every hand.

The Loss of Brotherly Love

Weaknesses in the Puritan experiment also began to appear when outsiders, such as Quakers and Baptists, who held different theological views, migrated into their region. They responded harshly, feeling their way of life was being threatened and, perhaps, even undermined. On the one hand, their response is understandable because they and their parents had sacrificed so much and worked so hard to carve out a life in the New England wilderness. Should they now allow outsiders to undermine—with doctrines and practices with which they did not agree—what they had established?

On the other hand, their reaction to these outsiders, who insisted on spreading their teachings in their midst, was less than Christian. They not only banned the newcomers from their communities, but also, in some cases, they imprisoned them and, occasionally, they hanged them.

This harsh reaction highlighted two things. First, it betrayed the loss of spiritual life. Secondly, it exposed the inherent weakness of a social order in which the civil government has a stake in a particular church and uses its power to advance the doctrines and practices of that church. In this case in New England, it was the Congregational Church, the church of the Puritans, that was merged, or aligned, with their system of civil government.

In the end, the New England experience of church and state made it clear that that the idea held by Quakers and Baptists—that the civil government should not be aligned with any church—was the better choice. In the Quaker and Baptist ideal, the civil government should diligently protect the free expression of faith for all sects and denominations, while taking sides with none of them. Just over 100 years later, all of this would play into the formulation of the First Amendment (December 15, 1791) in which the Founders would state, "Congress shall make no law concerning the establishment of religion, nor hindering the free exercise thereof."

Even so, at the time, the Puritans' harsh treatment of outsiders indicated that they were now in a defensive mode, and the whole thing served to dampen spiritual vision and passion for reform. This led to a hardening of outward forms of both their church and civil government. So, the structures that Puritans had originally instituted to facilitate and preserve their vision of Christian reform now became the instruments by which later generations crushed dissent and squelched new expressions of revival and reform.

The Witchcraft Trials

When people live as nominal Christians, believing in the doctrines of the Bible but lacking the power of a personal relationship with God, they are unable to deal with attacks from the unseen world of Satan and demons. This was the case with the Puritans in the 1690s, when rumors began to spread of the practice of witchcraft in their midst, particularly in the town of Salem, Massachusetts.

Then, when unexplained accidents began to occur and cases of demon possession began to appear, they had neither the spiritual wisdom nor the spiritual power to deal with the situation. Although there were isolated cases of deliverance through prayer and fasting,[49] for the most part, the people reacted in fear and relied on the civil authorities to deal with the situation. So began the darkest period of Puritan history, the Salem Witchcraft Trials of 1692-1693, in which over 150 people were arrested. Eventually, 20 were found guilty and 19 were hanged for practicing witchcraft.

These proceedings have been magnified by those who hold the Puritans in distain, and they have used them to paint a negative picture of the Puritans in hopes of destroying their reputation and undermining their overwhelmingly positive influence in the founding of this nation. It should be noted, however, that these proceedings took place in one small, isolated New England town. To try to paint the entire Puritan experience with this broad brush shows either bias or gross ignorance of the situation.

Noll has pointed out that, compared with what was happening in Europe at the time, the actions of the Puritans were quite guarded. In fact, in Europe during this same period, hundreds of alleged witches were executed at the behest of both Catholics and Protestants.[50] Others have pointed out that witchcraft was, in fact, being practiced. This being the case, when unexplained accidents began to occur, many New Englanders reacted in fear by going after those whom they believed to be responsible, bringing them to trial.

In defense of the Puritans—without exonerating them—

---

[49] Peter Marshall and David Manuel, 237.
[50] Noll, 51.

Attorney William H. Cooke, in his excellent book, *Justice at Salem: Reexamining the Witchcraft Trials*, shows the importance of judging their actions within the context of their own worldview rather than the context of a secularized, 21st Century worldview.

It must also be pointed out that it was actually the protests of Puritan pastors, such as Increase Mather (1639-1723), that eventually ended the trials. Later, Judge Samuel Sewall (1652-1730), one of the magistrates who presided over the proceedings, made a public statement lamenting his actions, lest some innocent person had been condemned. He asked for God's forgiveness for himself and all New England.[51] Even so, a dark cloud of uncertainty and disillusionment fell over all of New England.

Prayers for a Divine Awakening

By the end of the 17th Century, the Puritan vision of being a "shining light" and a "city on a hill" for the churches of Europe seemed dim, indeed. A similar "falling away" had occurred among the churches of the Middle and Southern Colonies. Many of the existing churches were spiritually dead, and because of rapid population growth, many areas were without churches and pastors. Sabbath breaking, profanity, gambling, and lewdness were rampant.

As the colonies entered the 1700s, many ministers and laypeople expressed concern about the immorality and spiritual indifference that permeated the land and the churches. Calling it a "dead and barren time," one pastor wrote,

---

[51] Peter Marshall and David Manuel, 238-39.

The golden showers have been restrained; the influences of the Spirit suspended; the consequence has been that the gospel has not had any eminent success. Conversions have been rare and dubious; few sons and daughters have been born to God; and the hearts of Christians not so quickened, warmed, and refreshed under the ordinances, as they have been.[52]

The general spiritual condition was so bleak that calls for special times of prayer and fasting were issued throughout the colonies by both pastors and government officials. William Cooper (1693-1743), who was a pastor in New England, said that before the Awakening (1726) there was "a constant petition in our public prayers, from Sabbath to Sabbath, that God would pour out His Spirit upon us and revive his work in the midst of the years." He reported that most of the churches had "set apart days, wherein to seek the Lord by prayer and fasting." In addition, there were "annual fast days appointed by the government."[53]

Would God be faithful to answer the prayers of His people? Would He honor the faith and sacrifice of their forefathers and foremothers? Would He demonstrate that He had a plan for this land?

------

[52] Jonathan Edwards, *Jonathan Edwards on Revival* (Carlisle, PA: Banner of Truth Trust, 1994), 77.

[53] Jonathan Edwards, 77.

Chapter 5

The Vision Renewed as God Awakened His People

> The work of God, as it was carried on, and the number of true saints multiplied, soon made a glorious alteration in the town: so that in the spring and summer following, anno 1735, the town seemed to be full of the presence of God.
>
> *Jonathan Edwards (1703-1758)*

By 1726, when revival broke out in New Jersey among the Dutch Reformed, it was obvious that God was beginning to answer the prayers of the people. It began as the result of a young Dutch Reformed pastor, Theodore Frelinghuysen (1691-*c.* 1748), visiting his flock in their homes and boldly pointing out—both privately in person, and publicly from the pulpit—the spiritual apathy and unchristian behavior that he observed. He confronted them about the reality of sin and reminded them about the grace of the Gospel, calling upon them to take their faith seriously.

In the beginning, some taking offence, separated from him, but eventually his preaching bore fruit as a powerful revival spread among the churches he pastored. When George Whitefield visited that area a few years later, he acknowledged the work of Frelinghuysen and said of him,

> He is a worthy soldier of Jesus Christ and was the beginner of the great work which I trust the Lord is carrying on in these parts.[54]

Gilbert Tennent

One notable person influenced by Frelinghuysen was Gilbert Tennent (1703-1764), a Presbyterian pastor in the town of New Brunswick, New Jersey. Born in County Armagh in Ireland, he had immigrated with his parents and three brothers to America when he was 14. The family settled in Bucks County, Pennsylvania, where his father, William, took the pastorate of the Neshaminy Presbyterian Church. It was here that Gilbert and his brothers received the training that would prepare them to be among the most prominent preachers of the Great Awakening.

William Tennant (1673-1746), was a Biblical scholar, well-versed in Hebrew, Greek, and Latin, who had been trained at the University of Edinburgh. He was also a man of piety who emphasized the importance of a vital faith that is both known in the head and experienced in the heart. One of his first acts, after getting the family settled in their new home, was to erect a log building approximately twenty feet long

---

[54] George Whitefield, *George Whitefield's Journals* (Carlisle, PA: Banner of Truth Trust, 1960), 352.

and twenty feet wide where he began classes with thirteen students, including Gilbert and his three brothers. Years later, when George Whitefield visited the area and preached to approximately 3000 in the "meeting-house yard," he described the Log College as being like the "old school of the prophets." Many historians consider the Log College to be the forerunner of Princeton University.[55]

After graduating from the Log College, Gilbert was licensed by the Presbyterian Church to preach, and he settled into a pastorate in New Brunswick, New Jersey. Shortly after assuming this pastorate, Gilbert became deathly ill and wondered if his life might be over. Feeling that he had accomplished so little in his Christian service, Gilbert promised God that, if He would allow him just six more months, he would "stand upon the stage of the world, as it were, and plead more faithfully for his cause, and take more earnest pains for the salvation of souls."[56]

Gilbert regained his health and preached with new urgency. Boldly, he pointed out the hypocrisy and the shallowness of faith among his congregants, insisting on a true conversion experience rooted solely in faith in Jesus Christ. Gilbert's bold and urgent tone led some to refer to him as *A Son of Thunder*. Despite some opposition, overall a deep concern for their spiritual state gripped his congregation and affected the entire community.

During this time, Gilbert met Theodore Frelinghuysen and observed the revival occurring in his Dutch Reformed

---

[55] Earle E. Cairns, 366.

[56] David O. Beale, "The Log College," *Faith of Our Fathers: Scenes from American Church History*, Mark Sidwell, ed. (Greenville, SC: BJU Press, 1991), 40-43.

Churches. They were able to encourage each other, and revival intensified throughout the Middle Colonies (*i.e.*, New Jersey, Pennsylvania, New York, and Delaware). When George Whitefield (1714-1770) visited the area in 1739, he said of Gilbert, "He and his associates are now the burning and shining lights of this part of America."[57]

As the Awakening accelerated, Gilbert traveled to more and more communities, proclaiming the importance of a "new birth" through faith in Jesus Christ. Everywhere he went, multitudes were awakened to the fact that they could not trust in the religion of their parents, church membership, or their own good works. Instead, they became aware that they must put their faith completely in Christ. Gilbert also challenged the clergy with a scathing message entitled *The Danger of an Unconverted Ministry*. In it, he compared many Colonial church leaders to the Pharisees of Jesus' day — pious and proud in their own righteousness but opposing the genuine work of God in their midst.

On one of his preaching tours, George Whitefield met the Tennents. Recognizing their significant contribution to the Awakening, he asked Gilbert to embark on a preaching tour in order to "water the seed" everywhere that he himself had preached. Gilbert agreed and saw amazing response. One writer has said, "Preaching almost every day for three months," Tennent witnessed a "shaking among the dry bones."[58]

In December 1740, about three months after Whitefield had left Boston, Gilbert Tennant spent about three months there, ministering with astounding results. One eyewitness wrote,

---

[57] George Whitefield, *George Whitefield's Journals* (Carlisle, PA: Banner of Truth Trust, 1960), 347.

[58] David O. Beale, "The Log College," 40-43.

The December following Mr. G. Tennent arrived whose preaching was followed by still greater effects. On Monday, March 2, 1741, Mr. Tennent preached his farewell sermon to an extremely crowded and deeply affected audience. And now was a time such as we never knew. Mr. Cooper was wont to say, that more came to him in one week in deep concern about their souls, than in the whole twenty-four years of his previous ministry.[59]

Jonathan Edwards and Revival in New England

 As revival was spreading in the Middle Colonies, it also broke out among the descendants of the Puritans in New England. A leader in that region was Jonathan Edwards (1703-1758), the pastor of the Congregational Church in Northampton, Massachusetts. Deeply concerned by what he described as "the general deadness throughout the land," he and his wife, Sarah Pierpont Edwards (1710–1758), set themselves to seek God for a "revival of religion."[60]

Edwards was a child prodigy who entered Yale College at 13, graduating four years later as class valedictorian. He was a diligent student of Scripture, well-versed in the biblical languages and thoroughly prepared for the service

---

[59] Verna M. Hall, *The Christian History of the American Revolution* (San Francisco: The Foundation for Christian Education, 1976), 123.

[60] David S. Lovejoy, *Religious Enthusiasm and the Great Awakening* (Englewood Cliffs, NJ: Prentice Hall, 1969), 5.

of the Lord. When he became the pastor of Northampton congregation in 1729, he continued his studies for 13 hours daily. He and Sarah continued to pray fervently, and God answered in a remarkable way.

During the spring and summer of 1735, an awesome sense of the Divine Presence could be felt throughout the entire community of Northampton. Edwards reported, "The town seemed to be full of the presence of God." In every part of town, the Spirit of God was powerfully at work until "there was scarcely a single person in the town, old or young, left unconcerned about the great things of the eternal world."[61]

Without any sort of planned evangelistic outreach "souls did as it were come by flocks to Jesus Christ." Instead of going to the tavern, people crowded Edwards' home, clamoring to hear the message of Christ and His salvation. As Edwards put it, his home "was thronged far more than ever the tavern had been wont to be." In fact, the Spirit of God worked so powerfully that "the tavern was soon left empty."[62] "A loose, careless person could scarcely be found," said Edwards, "and if there was anyone that seemed to remain senseless or unconcerned it would be spoken of as a *strange* thing."[63]

With no emphasis on church growth methods or other human attempts to increase attendance, the church in Northampton filled with those already born again and with others seeking salvation. Edwards wrote,

> Our public assemblies were then beautiful: the congregation was alive in God's service, everyone

---

[61] Jonathan Edwards, *Jonathan Edwards on Revival.* (Carlisle, PA: The Banner of Truth Trust), 13.

[62] Edwards, 24.

[63] Edwards, 19.

intent on the public worship, every hearer eager to drink in the words of the minister as they came from his mouth; the assembly were in general from time to time in tears while the word was preached; some weeping with sorrow and distress, others with joy and love, others with pity and concern for the souls of their neighbors.[64]

People from other communities often scoffed when they heard of the events in Northampton. But for many, this skepticism dissipated when they visited Northampton and personally experienced the overwhelming sense of God's presence. Edwards wrote,

Strangers were generally surprised to find things so much beyond what they had heard, and were wont to tell others that the state of the town could not be conceived by those who had not seen it.[65]

The Awakening spread. In some cases, visitors returning home carried the spirit of revival with them. In other cases, the Awakening spontaneously sprang up in communities having no apparent contact with Northampton. For example, the entire town of Hatfield was "seized with concern" about the things of God and salvation through Jesus Christ. And in Sunderland, the revival soon "overspread the town." In Westfield, a Rev. Bull told Edwards about the transformation of his town, saying "more had been done in one week than in seven years before."[66]

At this time, Edwards preached his famous sermon, *Sinners*

---

[64] Edwards, 14.
[65] Edwards, 14.
[66] Edwards, 16.

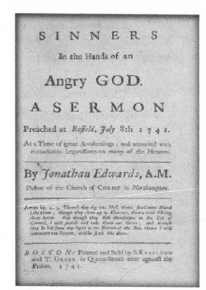

in the Hands of an Angry God in Enfield, Connecticut. As he preached, the justice of God and the reality of eternal punishment became so real to the congregation that some clutched the backs of pews while others wrapped their arms around the pillars to keep from falling into hell, as it were, and being consumed by its eternal flames. Prayers and loud cries for mercy from the congregation drowned Edwards' voice. "He made hell real enough to be found in the atlas," said Edwards' biographer, Ola Winslow.[67]

We might be tempted to think that Edwards' preaching style contributed to such a spectacle. But that was not the case! In fact, he was neither loud nor flamboyant in his delivery. Instead, true to his logical and studious personality, he would simply read aloud his meticulously written manuscript in a monotone voice, as he stood immovable behind the podium, making no gestures. Because he was nearsighted, he held his manuscript so close that the congregation could not see his face. (Perhaps this can serve to caution us today, not to mistake the noise and pizazz of contemporary Christian entertainment with the power of the Holy Spirit.)

It should be pointed out that preaching on the terrors of hell did not monopolize Edwards' messages. Instead, he spoke

---

[67] William Sweet, *Revivalism in America* (New York: Abingdon, 1944), 30.

much about the majesty of God and the excellence of Christ. He was, in fact, a very sensitive person who could be melted to tears while contemplating the love and mercy of God.

According to one report, before presenting his sermon, *Sinners in the Hands of an Angry God*, he had spent 18 hours in prayer, pleading with God: "Give me New England or let me die."[68] When Whitefield preached in the Northampton church, he noted in his *Journal*, "The good Mr. Edwards wept throughout the sermon."[69]

Isaac Watts (1674-1748), the English pastor, theologian, and hymn writer, read Edwards' account of how the Awakening had transformed New England and was greatly inspired. He wrote,

> We are taught by this happy event how easy it will be for our blessed Lord to make a full accomplishment of all His predictions concerning His kingdom, and to spread His dominion from sea to sea, through all the nations of the earth. We see how easy it is for Him with one turn of His hand, with one word of His mouth, to awaken whole countries of stupid and sleeping sinners, and kindle divine life in their souls.[70]

---

[68] *Change the Word School of Prayer* (Studio City, CA: World Literature Crusade, 1976), D-38.

[69] George Whitefield, 477.

[70] Jonathan Edwards, 3.

Chapter 6

The Marginalized of Society Are Awakened

The power of God seemed to descend upon the assembly
'like a might raging wind,' and with an astonishing energy
bore down all before it. They were almost universally praying
and crying in every part of the house, and many out of doors;
and numbers could neither go nor stand.
Their concern was so great, each one for himself,
that none seemed to take any notice of those about them,
but each prayed freely for himself.
I thought this had a near resemblance of the day
of God's power, mentioned in Josh. 10:14;
for I must say I never saw any day like it.

David Brainerd (1718 – 1747)
describing the Awakening
among the Delaware Indians of New Jersey

The preachers of the Great Awakening saw all people—
regardless of social status, race or gender—as being
under the power and penalty of sin, with only one remedy:

faith in Jesus Christ. In other words, whether a person was of high or low standing in society, rich or poor, male or female, slave or free was irrelevant when it came to forgiveness of sins through faith in Jesus Christ. Moved by this theological understanding and stirred by the power of the Awakening, many reached across cultural divides to share the Good News with those who had been relegated to the margins of Colonial American society. As a result, women, African Americans, and Native Americans shared in the liberating, elevating, saving power of the Awakening.

The Awakening Impacts Women

One writer has pointed out that, although critics of the Awakening took umbrage at emotional excesses, they believed they observed, they were even more incensed when "some white women and African Americans shed their subordinate social status long enough to exhort religious gatherings."[71]

A case in point is Sarah Pierpont Edwards (1710-1758), wife of Jonathan Edwards. The Awakening in Northampton had a powerful effect on her. At times, because of the overwhelming presence of God, she was unable to stand. At other times, she was so conscious of the joyful presence of the Holy Spirit, she says, "I could scarcely refrain from leaping with transports of joy." [72]

This sort of experience of the Holy Spirit's presence also moved her to act outside her traditional roles of wife and mother. She discussed Biblical and theological themes with

---

[71] Christine Leigh Heyrman, "The First Great Awakening," http://nationalhumanitiescenter.org/tserve/eighteen/ekeyinfo/grawaken.htm.

[72] Serno E. Dwight, *The Life of President Edwards* (New York: G. & C. & H. Carvill, 1830), 176-78.

her husband and visiting ministers, and she exhorted others out of the overflow of her own experience. On one occasion, she tells of hearing a visiting minister's lament that God's children should be so cold and lifeless in their faith. She said,

> I felt such a sense of the deep ingratitude manifested by the children of God, in such coldness and deadness, that my strength was immediately taken away, and I sunk down on the spot. Those who were near raised me, and placed me in a chair; and, from the fullness of my heart, I expressed to them, in a very earnest

> manner, the deep sense I had of the wonderful grace of Christ towards me, of the assurance I had of his having saved me from hell, of my happiness running parallel with eternity, of the duty of giving up all to God, and of the peace and joy inspired by an entire dependence on his mercy and grace.[73]

Remembering that Jonathan Edwards is considered by many to be the greatest theologian/philosopher America has produced, it is significant that his views on gender did not adhere to the cultural mold of his day. His commentary on Genesis 3:20, where Eve is called "the mother of all living," shows definite strains of gender equality.[74] Perhaps the fact that he grew up with ten siblings—all sisters—had a bearing on his thinking. His letters reveal an affection and respect for his sisters, all of whom attended

---

[73] Dwight, 177.

[74] Anthony, Uyl, *The Works of Jonathan Edwards I – II* (Woodstock, ON: Devoted Publ., 2017), 154.

college, something rare for that day and age. His older sisters also helped tutor him, preparing him for college.

There is no question, however, that the greatest female influence in life was his wife, Sarah, whom he considered a model of purity and grace. He and Sarah apparently raised their daughters with a sense of their being equal with men, for one biographer, in describing the character of their daughter, Esther, said, "She was used to being taken seriously as the spiritual and intellectual equal of men."

These trends toward equality are, in fact, always observable in movements of spiritual renewal. In such times, more value is placed on the Spirit's manifest presence and power for teaching and ministry than is placed on more traditional, cultural, and religious criteria, such as whether God's chosen vessel is male or female.

This expression of gender equality, readily demonstrated by the Quakers, for example, was rooted both in their observation of the activity of the Holy Spirit and in their understanding of Scripture. To a lesser extent, women were also elevated among the Baptists of Colonial America. But traditional, Puritan culture and theology that was dominant at the time, especially in New England, confined women almost exclusively to the domestic sphere, where they were expected to fulfill only roles of motherhood and homemaker. Freedom was confined within these roles.[75]

Even so, through the influence of the Great Awakening, the way opened for women to play some very prominent roles

---

[75] For a thorough discussion of this phenomena see Susan Hyatt, In the Spirit We're Equal (Dallas: Hyatt Press, 1998).

in the American Revolution (1775–1783).[76] Also, it generated ripples of equality that would grow into a spiritual *tsunami* in the Second Great Awakening (*c.a.* 1800–1830s), and out that would emerge the Suffrage Movement and the great fight for both gender and racial equality.[77]

The Awakening Impacts Native Americans

Relationships between the Colonists and the Native Americans of the region had become strained. This was caused, on the one hand, by the lust for land on the part of second and third generation immigrants. On the other hand, it was caused by fear and mistrust on the part of the native chiefs and medicine men who saw the settlers and their religion as threats to their own power and influence. By the late 1600s, these tensions erupted into brutal conflicts, and the chasm between the two peoples widened. Nevertheless, moved by the power of the Awakening and by its central theme that all people are separated from God by sin and stand in need of salvation through Christ, a number of ardent souls began to reach out in genuine kindness and at great personal sacrifice, to the Native Americans. As a result, a powerful work of the Holy Spirit occurred among the native people.

A case in point is David Brainerd (1718-1747), who worked with the Mohicans, Stockbridge, and Susquehanna in Massachusetts, and with the Delaware in New Jersey and Pennsylvania. His missionary career was cut short by tuberculosis and his death at the age of 29 in the Edwards' home. Nevertheless, his

---

[76] David Barton, "Glenn Beck," Fox News Channel, May 27, 2011.

[77] See Timothy Smith, *Revivalism and Social Reform in Mid-Nineteenth Century America*, in which he shows that modern civil rights movements have their roots in American revivalism.

missionary dedication became an inspiring example to many, especially after Jonathan Edwards published his *Journal* following his passing.

Brainerd gave himself completely and sacrificially to his task.

BRAINERD PREACHING TO THE INDIANS.

Among other things, this meant learning the native languages to a level of competency that enabled him to share portions of the Gospels and the Psalms in those languages. Also, in the wilderness, where he was often alone and without basic sustenance, he gave himself to fervent prayer for the people and often set aside entire days for prayer and fasting.

His *Journal* entry for April 19, 1742, reads:

I set apart this day for fasting and prayer to God for his grace; especially to prepare me for the work of the ministry; to give me divine aid and direction in my preparations for that great work; and in his own time to send me into his harvest. In the forenoon I felt the power of intercession for precious, immortal souls; for the advancement of the kingdom of my dear Lord and Savior in the world . . . God enabled me so to agonize in prayer that I was quite wet with sweat, though in the shade and the cool wind. My soul was drawn out very much for the world; I grasped for multitudes of souls (April 19, 1742).

While ministering to the Delaware Tribe in Crossweeksung,

New Jersey, in 1745, Brainerd began to see remarkable answers to his petitions. His *Journal* entry on August 8, 1745, reads:

> The power of God seemed to descend upon the assembly 'like a mighty raging wind,' and with an astonishing energy bore down all before it. I stood amazed at the influence which seized the audience almost universally; and could compare it to nothing more aptly than the irresistible force of a mighty torrent, or swelling deluge, that with its insupportable weight and pressure bears down and sweeps before it whatever is in its way. The most stubborn hearts were now obliged to bow. A principal man among the Indians . . . was now brought under solemn concern for his soul and wept bitterly. They were almost universally praying and crying for mercy in every part of the house, and many out of doors; and numbers could neither go nor stand. Their concern was so great, each one for himself, that none seemed to take any notice of those about them, but each prayed freely for himself. I thought this had a near resemblance to the day of God's power, mentioned in Josh. 10: 14; for I must say I never saw any day like it, in all respects: it was a day wherein I am persuaded the Lord did much to destroy the kingdom of darkness among this people.[78]

His work bore much good fruit among the Delaware. A thriving Christian community and church emerged, and because he raised money to help secure their land, they were guaranteed that it would never be taken from them.

---

[78] Richard A. Hasler, *Journey with David Brainerd* (Downers Grove: InterVarsity Press, 1975), 80-81.

Of his beloved Native American congregation, he wrote,

> I know of no assembly of Christians, where there seems to be so much of the presence of God, where brotherly love so much prevails, and where I should take so much delight in the public worship of God in general, as in my own congregation.[56]

Brainerd died of tuberculosis two years later, and others, including his brother, John, carried on his work. John Wesley was so moved by his reading of Brainerd's *Journal*, that he had it distributed to all of his Methodist societies, instructing his preachers, "Read carefully over the life of David Brainerd." Jonathan Edwards also extended Brainerd's influence, expressing deep appreciation for his life and work. And perhaps, as further fruit of his example, Edwards himself became a missionary to the Housatonic Indians of the Stockbridge, Massachusetts, region.

As a result of all of these efforts, the Colonists had a good working relationship with many native peoples. This proved strategic when the Revolutionary War broke out in 1775. On the one hand, the British were able to persuade many tribes to join their side of the conflict through promises of land guarantees and claims of military superiority and certain victory over the Colonists. On the other hand, because of the established rapport, a substantial contingent of Native Americans sided with the Colonists. Interestingly, many of these people were from the areas where Brainerd, Edwards, and others had seen the most success, such as Stockbridge, in western Massachusetts, and throughout New England. Also, further south and west, in a region where Presbyterian missionary, Samuel Kirkland (1741–1808) had labored, the Oneida and Tuscarora sided with the Colonists. Some volunteered as Minutemen even before the outbreak of the fighting. Other joined Washington's army at the Siege of Boston (April 17, 1775 - March 17, 1776), and others served in New York, New Jersey, and other regions of conflict.[79]

The Awakening Impacts African Americans

Because of the understanding that all people are under the power of sin and in need of Christ, a number of evangelists of the Awakening targeted African Americans, both slave and free, in their preaching. The message of a personal new birth experience with God resonated with these people. Also, they found specific parts of the Biblical narrative with which they could closely identify, such as Israel's time of slavery in Egypt and God's mighty deliverance of His people.

The historical record shows a Great Awakening among African Americans. For example, Gilbert Tennent expresses great delight in his report of a preaching tour in Massachusetts. He writes, "Multitudes were awakened, and several received great consolation, especially among the young people, children, and 'Negroes.'"[80] Also, Jonathan Edwards, in his account of the Awakening in Northampton, mentions "several negroes" who appeared to have been born again.[81]

Meanwhile, further south, Samuel Davies (1723-1761), who was a colleague of Gilbert Tennent, gave special attention to African-Americans, both slave and free, during his time of

---

[79] Collin G. Calloway, "American Indians and the American Revolution," http://www.nps.gov/revwar/about_the_revolution/american_indians.html

[80] Noll, 106.

[81] Edwards, 20.

ministry in Virginia. Davies not only preached to them, but he also invited them to share in regular church observances, including the Lord's Supper. In 1757, he wrote,

> What little success I have lately had, has been chiefly among the extremes of Gentlemen and Negroes. Indeed, God has been remarkably working among the latter. I have baptized 150 adults; and at the last sacramental solemnity, I had the pleasure of seeing the table graced with 60 black faces.[82]

George Whitefield also testifies to the response of African Americans in his meetings. For example, after preaching his farewell message in Philadelphia and retiring to his lodging, he reported that, "Near 50 Negroes came to give me thanks for what God had done for their souls." Whitefield considered this an answer to prayer, saying, "I have been much drawn in prayer for them, and have seen them wrought upon by the word preached."[83]

On one occasion, a black woman who had been converted under Whitefield's ministry became discouraged and prayed that the Lord would manifest Himself to her. Shortly thereafter, both she and Whitefield were in a meeting where a Baptist minister was preaching. Whitefield said that the word came with such power that the woman began to cry out and, "could not help praising and blessing God."

When some criticized this woman for interrupting the preacher, Whitefield came to her defense saying he believed that, in that hour, "the Lord Jesus took a great possession of her soul." He went on to say, "I doubt not, when the poor Negroes are

---

[82] Noll, 106-07.
[83] Whitefield, 422.

to be called, God will highly favor them, to wipe off their reproach, and show that He is no respecter of persons."[84]

Whitfield was passionate about reaching the black population of Colonial America with the Gospel. In his travels, he reached out to blacks, both slave and free. In his *Journal*, he tells of stopping for the night at an estate that owned slaves. When he insisted on meeting the slaves and their families, his hosts were reluctant at first, but finally agreed. He then spent a very edifying time conversing and praying with the slaves and their children. He was especially impressed with how the children followed him in prayer, and afterwards he wrote in his *Journal*,

> This more and more convinces me that negro children, if early brought up in the virtue and admonition of the Lord, would make as great proficiency as any white people's children. I do not despair, if God spares my life, of seeing a school of young negroes singing the praises of Him who made them.[85]

Whitefield's impact among the black population of Colonial America is illustrated by the moving tribute that a young black woman by the name of Phillis Wheatley (1753-1784) wrote at the time of his death in 1770. No doubt, she had attended his meetings when he preached in Boston and may have been converted under his ministry.

Wheatley, who became America's first published black poet, was 17 years old when she wrote the poem about Whitefield. Her words express the strains of equality she heard in the Gospel he preached. They also express the inherent power

---

[84] Whitefield, 420.
[85] Whitefield, 379.

of the Gospel to lift the lowliest and to infuse them with a sense of eternal significance. Her poem reads, in part:

> *Thou didst in strains of eloquence refined,*
> *Inflame the heart and captivate the mind.*
> *The greatest gift that even God can give,*
> *He freely offered to the numerous throng,*
> *Take him, ye Africans, he longs for you,*
> *Impartial Savior is his title due.*
> *Washed in the fountain of Redeeming blood,*
> *You shall be sons and kings, and Priests to God.*[86]

In this, her first published poem, Wheatley quoted directly from Whitefield. It is easy to imagine him crying out to the blacks in his audience, "Take him, ye Africans! He longs for you!" This was likely the case in one of his Philadelphia meetings in in which his message left many blacks weeping and in awe. One black woman said that he must have been in a trance and insisted, "Jesus Christ must have told him what to speak to the people or else he could not speak as he did."[87]

The Cultural Chasm Is Breached

It is obvious that, in these revival meetings, blacks and whites were worshiping together. This should not be surprising, for

---

[86] Mark Noll, *A History of the United States and Canada* (Grand Rapids: Eerdmans, 1992), 109.

[87] Hyatt, *Pilgrims and Patriot*, 95.

in genuine spiritual awakening, the Holy Spirit breaks down racial and cultural barriers, and this occurred in the Great Awakening. Mark Noll, Professor of Church History at Wheaton College, confirms this: "It was under the impulse of the revival that the chasm between white and black cultures was breached."[88]

This Awakening among African Americans resulted in the emergence of black congregations, both slave and free. It also opened the way for African Americans to serve in the Revolutionary War, for it was, no doubt, the influence of the Awakening that led Washington to order his recruiting officers to accept free blacks into the ranks of the Continental Army. By 1781, one in every seven soldiers was black.[89] David Barton has provided documentation showing that numbers of blacks were given honorable discharges and pensions, and that some were honored with complete military funerals for their service in the Revolutionary War.[90]

Although at this early stage, the emphasis was on evangelism, the Awakening created a climate out of which moral outrage burst forth against the institution of slavery. The opposition to slavery, in fact, eventually became so strong in the North that when the separation from England came in 1776, several states, including Pennsylvania, Massachusetts, Connecticut, Rhode Island, Vermont, New Hampshire, and New York, immediately took steps to abolish slavery, something they could not do under King George III.

---

[88] Noll, 107.

[89] Thomas Fleming, "George Washington: The Forgotten Emancipator," https://historynewsnetwork.org/article/151759

[90] David Barton, "Glen Beck," The Fox News Channel, May 27, 2011.

Although there was more resistance in the South, the anti-slavery sentiments let loose by the Awakening flowered into the Abolition Movement of the next century, which, as Dr. Timothy Smith has shown, had its roots in American Revivalism, starting with the First Great Awakening.[91]

---

[91] See Timothy Smith, *Revivalism and Social Reform in Mid-Nineteenth Century America* (New York City: Harper & Rowe, 1965).

Chapter 7

The Nationalization of the Awakening

Speaking of George Whitefield,
Benjamin Franklin remarked:

The multitudes of all sects and denominations
that attended his sermons were enormous,
and it was a matter of speculation to me,
who was one of the number, to observe
the extraordinary influence of his oratory on his hearers.

From being thoughtless or indifferent about religion,
it seemed as if all the world were growing religious
so that one could not walk through the town
in an evening without hearing
psalms sung in different families of every street.

Benjamin Franklin (1706-1790)

George Whitefield (1714–1770) was uniquely prepared for his role as the firebrand of the Awakening that would bring all the individual flames of revival together into one Divine blaze of Spiritual Awakening. He was a graduate of Oxford University and an ordained minister in the Church of England. While at Oxford, he met John and Charles Wesley and became a part of the Holy Club, out of which came the Methodist Revival.[92]

Also, while at Oxford, he had become aware of his own corrupt nature. As a result, he spent much time wrestling in prayer and study until he finally came to a place of inner peace. That peace had come when he trusted himself to Jesus Christ completely. From that point forward, he had an insatiable hunger for God's Word. Later, he described this life-changing experience:

> My mind now being more open and enlarged, I began to read the Holy Scriptures upon my knees, laying aside all other books and praying over, if possible, every line and word."[93]

When he was 21, he was ordained to the Anglican ministry by Dr. Benson, the Bishop of Gloucester. When hands were

---

[92] The Methodist Revival was instigated by the preaching of Whitefield after he was ordained by the Church of England. The Wesley brothers were in Georgia at the time. Upon their return to England and Whitefield's departure for America, John Wesley and his brother Charles became the leaders of the revival in England. They all remained officially within the Anglican Church, but their desire for genuine spiritual renewal and their diligent study of the New Testament opened them to other communities of faith. After John Wesley's death in 1791, the leaders of the Methodist Revival met and formed themselves into an institution called the Methodist Church.

[93] Whitefield, 60.

laid on him at that time, he remembered, "My heart was melted down, and I offered up my whole spirit, soul and body, to the service of God's sanctuary."[94]

Because he was cross-eyed, Whitefield's critics called him *Dr. Squintum*. Nevertheless, his gifted preaching drew great crowds and quickly launched him into leadership of the Methodist Revival in England, alongside John and Charles Wesley. Sensing a divine call to the Colonies, he embarked on his first of seven visits in 1738, arriving in Savannah, Georgia, on May 7. He went with a burden for the Colonists and with a prayer that they would not live as thirteen scattered colonies, but as *one nation under God*.[95]

Entire Communities Are Transformed

So effective was his ministry, that, as he travelled up and down the Eastern Seaboard, shopkeepers closed their doors, farmers left their plows, and workers threw down their tools to hurry to the place where he was to preach. Crowds of 8,000-10,000 were common. At a time when the population of Boston was estimated to be 17,000, Whitefield preached to an estimated crowd of 20,000 on the Boston Common. Through his continuous travels, he became the best known and most recognized figure in Colonial America.

When Whitefield preached in Middletown, Connecticut, Nathan Cole, a farmer, gave a vivid description of the stir it caused throughout the region. Cole was working in his field, twelve miles away in Kensington, when a passerby told him

---

[94] Whitefield, 61.

[95] http://www.washingtonubf.org/ Resources/Leaders/GeorgeWhitefield.html.

that Whitefield would be preaching in Middletown at 10 o'clock that same morning.

Cole immediately dropped his tools, ran to the house, and told his wife to get ready to go to hear Whitefield preach. He then saddled their horse. They both mounted, and they hurried on their way to Middletown. Concerned that the horse might tire carrying two riders that distance, Cole would ride for a while and then dismount and run alongside.

As the Coles approached the junction of the main road from Hartford to Middletown, they saw an amazing sight. A cloud of dust rose above the hills and trees, and they heard a sound like a low rumble of thunder. As they drew closer, they realized that the dust and sound were caused by a huge company of horses and riders on their way to hear Whitefield preach. No one made a sound and there was something surreal about the scene as every rider seemed somber and intent on his purpose. "It made me tremble to see the sight," said Cole. He went on to say:

When we got to the Middletown old meeting house there was a great multitude, which was said to be three or four thousand people assembled together. I turned and looked towards the great river and saw the ferry boats running swift bringing over loads of people. The land and banks over the river looked black with people and horses all along the 12 miles. I saw no man at work in his field, but all seemed to be gone. When I saw Mr. Whitefield come upon the scaffold, he looked almost angelical; a young, slim, slender youth before some thousands of people with a bold undaunted countenance. And my hearing how God was with him everywhere he came along, it solemnized my mind and put me into a trembling fear before he began to preach, for he looked as if he was clothed with authority from the Great God, and a sweet, solemn solemnity sat upon his brow. And my hearing him preach gave me a heart wound. By God's blessings, my old foundation was broken up, and I saw that my righteousness would not save me.[96]

Whitefield and Benjamin Franklin (1706-1790) became friends, and Whitefield stayed as a guest in Franklin's home on at least one his seven visits to America. In his *Autobiography*, Franklin tells of the remarkable change that came over Philadelphia as a result of Whitefield's visit. He wrote,

In 1739 there arrived among us from Ireland the Reverend Mr. Whitfield who made himself remarkable there as an itinerant preacher. He was at first permitted to preach in some of our churches, but the clergy, taking a dislike to him, soon refused him their pulpits, and he was obliged to preach in the fields. The multitudes of all sects and denominations that attended his sermons were enormous, and it was a matter of speculation to me, who was one of the number, to observe the extraordinary influence of his oratory on his hearers. It was wonderful to see the change soon made in the manners of our inhabitants. From being thoughtless or indifferent about religion, it seemed as if all the world were growing religious so that one could not walk through the town in an evening without hearing psalms sung in different families of every street.[97]

---

[96] George Whitefield's Journals, 560-562.

[97] Benjamin Franklin, *The Autobiography of Benjamin Franklin* (New York City: Airmont Publishing, 1965), 100.

Franklin admits that he was initially skeptical of reports of Whitefield's preaching being heard by crowds of 25,000 and more. So, with his enquiring, scientific mind, he devised a way to settle it for himself. On one occasion, when Whitefield was preaching to a huge crowd from the top of the Philadelphia Courthouse steps, Franklin stepped off the distance to which Whitefield's voice could be heard. He then calculated that Whitefield's voice, which he described as "loud and clear" could, in fact, be heard by crowds of 30,000 and more.[98]

The Awakening Touches All Sects and Denominations.

Although ordained by the Church of England, Whitefield did not have a denominational bone in his body. A story from one of his sermons helps to illustrate this. One day, when he was preaching to several thousand gathered in the open air, he engaged in an imaginary conversation between himself and Father Abraham, whom he portrayed as looking over the banister of heaven at the multitude of people from many different sects and denominations.

Whitefield shouted, "Father Abraham, are there any Anglicans in heaven?" The answer came back, "No, there are no Anglicans in heaven." "Father Abraham, are there any Methodists in heaven?" "No, there are no Methodists in heaven." "Are there any Presbyterians in heaven?" "No, there are no Presbyterians here either." "What about Baptists or Quakers?" "No, there are none of those here either." "Father Abraham," shouted Whitefield, "what kind of people are in heaven?" The answer came back, "There are only Christians in heaven; only those

---

[98] Benjamin Franklin, 103.

who are washed in the blood of the Lamb." Whitefield then exclaimed, "Oh, is that the case? Then God, help me, God, help us all, to forget having names and to become Christians in deed and in truth!"[99]

The Christ-centered preaching of Whitefield broke down sectarian and denominational walls, so much so that a British-appointed official wrote to his superiors in England, "If you ask an American who is his master, he will tell you he has none, nor any governor but Jesus Christ."[100]

The Holy Spirit Is Poured Out

Everywhere Whitefield went, the Holy Spirit was poured out in great power. On one occasion after preaching to a huge crowd gathered outdoors, he paused to survey the crowd, later describing what he saw:

> Look where I would, most were drowned in tears. Some were struck pale as death, others wringing their hands, others lying on the ground, others sinking into the arms of their friends and most lifting up their eyes to heaven and crying out to God.[101]

In a meeting in Delaware, there was such an outpouring that Whitefield himself was overcome, along with many in the audience. He wrote,

> Never did I see a more glorious sight. Oh, what tears were shed and poured forth after the Lord Jesus. Some fainted; and when they had got a little strength, they

---

[99] Peter Marshall and David Manuel, 248.

[100] Peter Marshall and David Manuel, 267.

[101] *George Whitefield's Journals,* 425.

would hear and faint again. Others cried out in a manner as if they were in the sharpest agonies of death. After I had finished my last discourse, I was so pierced, as it were, and over-powered with a sense of God's love, that some thought, I believe, I was about to give up the ghost. How sweetly did I lie at the feet of Jesus.[102]

Whitefield's Message

Whitefield emphasized that many professing Christians had built their faith on faulty foundations, such as good deeds, church membership, cultural refinement, family pedigree, and social status. He emphasized that these old foundations must be overturned and that faith in Jesus Christ alone must be laid as the only foundation for acceptance with God.

He brought this vividly to the minds of a large audience as

---

[102] Whitefield, 425.

he preached on the parable of the ten virgins from Matthew 25:1-13. He pointed out that all ten were virgins and all had lamps, which he said symbolized their outward profession. Only the five wise virgins, however, had oil in their lamps, which Whitfield said symbolized a new heart brought about by a living faith in Christ alone. He told of the five foolish virgins knocking at the door of the wedding but being turned away by the Lord.

> "Lord, Lord," say they, as though they were intimately acquainted with the holy Jesus. Like numbers among us who, because they go to church, repeat their creeds, and receive the blessed sacrament, think they have a right to call Jesus their Savior and dare call God their Father, when they put up the Lord's Prayer. But Jesus is not your Savior. The devil, not God, is your father, unless your hearts are purified by faith and you are born again from above. It is not merely being baptized with water, but being born again of the Holy Ghost that must qualify you for salvation; and it will do you no service at that great day, to say unto Christ, "Lord, my name is in the register of such and such parish." I am persuaded the foolish virgins could say this and more.[103]

This emphasis on the interior condition of the heart before God, rather than on outward, religious formality, was characteristic, not only of Whitefield, but also of all the preachers of the Great Awakening. This emphasis found its way into the culture of America and has been expressed by many, such as Abraham Lincoln, who never joined a church

---

[103] George Whitefield, *Sermons of George Whitefield* (Peabody, MA: Hendrickson, 2009), 107.

but often prayed and exhibited a deep faith in the God of the Bible.

Staying on Message

Although outward manifestations, such as falling, trembling, weeping, and crying out, were common in Whitefield's meetings, he neither encouraged nor discouraged them. He was aware that when the Holy Spirit is manifest in remarkable and unusual ways, there may be genuine but unusual responses from many. Even so, as early as 1739, he had cautioned John Wesley not to over-emphasize outward manifestations, lest the people become preoccupied with them and so be led away from the truths of God's Word. He wrote,

> I think it is tempting God to require such signs. That there is something of God in it, I doubt not. But the devil, I believe, does interpose. I think it will encourage the French Prophets, take people away from the written word, and make them depend on visions, convulsions, etc., more than on the promises and precepts of the gospel.[104]

Although British, Whitefield is most remembered for his ministry in America during the First Great Awakening. Travelling from Georgia to Maine, he preached and raised support for Bethesda, his orphanage in Georgia. No doubt his hectic, demanding schedule brought about his death when he was 56 and visiting America for the seventh time.

---

[104] Arnold A. Dallimore, *George Whitefield. The Life and Times of the Great Evangelist of the Eighteenth-Century Revival* (Westchester, IL: Cornerstone Books, 1979), 1:328.

The cause of his passing was probably congestive heart failure, brought on by fatigue.

Whitfield Burns Out for God

As he entered his 56th year, Whitefield was experiencing chest pains and difficulty breathing. Worn out from his unceasing labors, but moved by a sense of urgency, he continued his demanding schedule. After preaching in Boston in September of 1770, and in spite of pain and weariness, he traveled on and prepared to preach to a large crowd in an open field near Newburyport, Massachusetts.

Someone, noticing his worn and haggard appearance, said to him, "Sir, you are more fit to go to bed, than to preach." "True," he responded, and then he prayed aloud,

> Lord Jesus, I am weary *in* Thy work, but not *of* it. If I have not finished my course, let me go and speak for Thee once more in the fields, and seal Thy truth, and come home and die.[105]

He then preached with great freedom and power for upwards of two hours, and then then retired to the home of a friend, Rev. Jonathan Parsons, to spend the night. Hundreds followed him to the parsonage, however, desiring to hear more of the goodness and grace of God in Jesus Christ.

Although weary, Whitefield emerged with a candle, as night had fallen. He told the crowed he would pray and preach until the candle went out. He then poured out his heart until the candle finally burned down and went out.

---

[105] Peter Marshall and David Manuel, 252.

He then dismissed the crowd and went inside and went to bed.

His sleep, however, was restless and he awakened in the middle of the night. He talked with his hosts and went back to sleep, but he awakened later with a tight chest and difficulty breathing. He finally stopped breathing altogether and despite a doctor's attempts to revive him, he expired at 6 a.m. on September 30, 1770.

Offers to bury him came from New Hampshire and from Boston's Old South Church. Parsons, however, arranged for Whitefield's interment in the vault, underneath the pulpit, of the Newburyport Presbyterian Church. His remains are still there today.

America Was Never the Same

Daniel Rogers, who had been converted under Whitefield's ministry thirty years before and who had remained a loyal friend, prayed at the funeral. He said that he owed his conversion "to the labors of that dear man of God, whose precious remains now lay before them." Rogers then began weeping and crying out, "O my father, my father!" The congregation melted into tears.[106]

Condolences poured in from throughout the Colonies and from Great Britain. Franklin was in London at the time of Whitefield's death. When he received word of his friend's passing, he wrote:

I knew him intimately upwards of thirty years; his

---

[106] Thomas S. Kidd, *George Whitefield: America's Spiritual Founding Father* (New Haven: Yale University Press, 2014), 251.

integrity, disinterestedness, and indefatigable zeal in prosecuting every good work, I have never seen equaled, I shall never see exceeded.[107]

As a result of Whitefield's "indefatigable zeal" in preaching the Gospel to Colonial America, neither America nor Franklin, the skeptical printer of Philadelphia, would ever be the same. This is why Whitefield is called *America's Spiritual Founding Father* by Thomas S. Kidd, Professor of History at Baylor University.

The Significance of Whitfield's Ministry

George Whitfield's role in preparing America for statehood was enormous. More than anyone else, because of his continuous travels, he brought the Colonies together and helped make the Awakening a national event. His meetings were the first events that brought together the scattered Colonists of various denominational and theological persuasions. Denominational walls came down, and for the first time, they saw themselves as a single people with one Divine destiny: *One Nation under God,* as Whitfield had prayed.

Hart points out that when Whitefield visited America for the final time in 1770, even the Episcopal churches, which had initially rejected him, opened their doors to him. Hart goes on to say,

> The true Spirit of Christ had dissolved sectarian differences. America considered itself to be a nation

---

[107] Kidd, 253.

of Christians, pure and simple, as Whitefield noted with satisfaction. "Pulpits, hearts and affections," he said, were opened to him and any preacher of whatever denomination who had a true Christian message to share.[108]

The preaching of Whitefield and other revivalists of the Great Awakening also helped democratize the Colonies by putting everyone on the same level: that being, guilty sinners before God with only one solution for the sin problem, and that being faith in Jesus Christ. They also helped to bridge the gap between clergy and laypeople by insisting that it was the responsibility of every individual to know God in a real and personal way. Furthermore, they encouraged their followers to carry out ordinances and activities that had traditionally been reserved for an ordained clergy.

There is no question that the preaching of Whitefield, Edwards, Frelinghuysen, the Tennents, and others paved the way for nationhood. As Harvard professor William Perry said, "The Declaration of Independence of 1776 was a result of the evangelical preaching of the evangelists of the Great Awakening."[109]

These same preachers also prepared the way for the abolition of slavery in America.

---

[108] Hart, 224.

[109] Lawrence LaCour, Lecture on "Ministry of Evangelism," Oral Roberts University, Fall 1989; quoted in Hyatt, 2000 Years of Charismatic Christianity (Lake Mary, FL: Charisma House, 2002), 112.

Chapter 8

The Attack on Slavery

> Blush ye pretended votaries of freedom! ye trifling Patriots!
> who are making a vain parade of being advocates
> for the liberties of mankind,
> who are thus making a mockery of your profession
> by trampling on the sacred natural rights
> and privileges of Africans.
>
> *John Allen, Baptist Preacher of the Great Awakening*

Dr. Walter E. Williams, the Professor of Economics at George Mason University, who is African American, points out that slavery in America was neither odd nor strange, for at the beginning of the 19th Century, "An estimated three-quarters of all people alive were trapped in bondage against their will either in some form of slavery or serfdom."[110] He also says that the unique characteristic of slavery in America was the "moral outrage" against it.

The brilliant historian, Dr. Thomas Sowell, who also happens to be African American, has made the same point. He notes that, although slavery has been a world-wide institution

---

[110] Walter E. Williams, "Slavery Is Neither Strange Nor Peculiar," https://www.creators.com/read/walter-williams/05/19/slavery-is-neither-strange-nor-peculiar

practiced by peoples and civilizations for thousands of years, it only became controversial in the 18th Century in Western civilization and particularly in America. He writes,

Slavery was just not an issue, not even among intellectuals, much less among political leaders, until the 18th century–and then it was an issue only in Western civilization. Among those who turned against slavery in the 18th century were George Washington, Thomas Jefferson, Patrick Henry and other American leaders. You could research all of the 18th century Africa or Asia or the Middle East without finding any comparable rejection of slavery there.[111]

The Source of This Moral Outrage

It was the Great Awakening that unleashed the anti-slavery sentiments and moral outrage that eventually brought an end to slavery on American soil. As a result of the Awakening, the racial chasm was breached, slaves were humanized, and whites were awakened to the evils of slavery. The Great Awakening, indeed, produced the "moral outrage" mentioned by Sowell and Williams, and it marked the beginning of the end of slavery in America.

---

[111] Thomas Sowell, "Twisted History," https://townhall.com/columnists/thomassowell/2003/12/17/twisted-history-n1057496

Early Revivalists Prepared the Way

At the beginning of the Awakening in 1726, outreach to the black population was evangelistic in nature; it was not characterized by opposition to slavery. The early preachers, such as Whitefield, Tennant, Edwards and others, saw their primary purpose to be in getting people ready for the next world, not necessarily improving their lot in this one. In their thinking, a slave on his way to heaven was far better off than a king on his way to hell.

Nonetheless, the message of those early evangelists had a levelling effect on American society. The message they preached applied to all, regardless of race, gender, or social class. All have sinned and fallen short of God's glory and all are in need of a Savior — and that Savior is Jesus Christ.

Their compassion for blacks, both slave and free, and their willingness to share Christian fellowship with them broke down racial and cultural barriers. Their preaching and actions created a climate conducive to the anti-slavery sentiments that would emerge from the preaching of those who came after them.

The Attack on Slavery Begins with the Congregationalists in New England

Descendants of the Puritans led the way in the attacks on slavery. Evangelists who came after Edwards and Whitefield carried the message of their predecessors to its logical conclusion: if we are all creatures of the same Creator and if Christ died that all might be saved, then how can slavery ever be justified?

Motivated by this fact, they began to attack the institution of slavery with passion. This is what historian, Benjamin Hart, was referring to when he wrote, "Among the most ardent opponents of slavery were ministers, particularly the Puritan and revivalist preachers."[112] These "ardent opponents of slavery" included the followers of Jonathan Edwards who expanded on his idea of the essential dignity of all created beings and applied it to the African slaves of Colonial America.

Samuel Hopkins (1721–1803), for example, who had been personally tutored by Edwards, pastored for a time in Newport, Rhode Island, an important hub in the transatlantic slave trade. His response to slavery in Newport was like Paul's response to the idols in Athens. Paul's spirit was "provoked" by the idols of the Athenians, and Hopkins was deeply stirred by the "violation of God's will" he saw in Newport. He declared, "This whole country have their hands full of blood this day."[113]

In 1774, after the First Continental Congress had convened in Philadelphia, Hopkins sent a pamphlet to every member of the Congress, asking how they could complain about "enslavement" to England and overlook the "enslavement" of so many blacks in the Colonies. *Liberty* was becoming a watchword throughout the Colonies, and the preachers of the Awakening began to apply it to the enslaved in America. Like Hopkins, they pointed out the hypocrisy of demanding freedom from England while continuing to uphold the institution of slavery in their midst.

---

[112] Hart. 330.

[113] Thomas S. Kidd, *God of Liberty* (New York: Basic Books, 2010), 153.

The opposition to slavery mounted as other ministers of the Awakening began to speak out, and Noll writes,

> In this attack on slavery, Hopkins was joined by other followers of Edwards, including Levi Hart in Connecticut, Jacob Green in New Jersey, and Edwards' own son, Jonathan, Jr., who was also a minister in Connecticut.[114]

The influence of these ministers spread to others in both business and government. For example, James Otis, Jr., a lawyer and member of the Massachusetts provincial assembly, called slavery "the most shocking violation of the law of nature" and a vice "that makes every dealer in it a petty tyrant."[115]

In a sermon preached and published in 1770, Samuel Cooke declared that by tolerating the evil of slavery, "We, the patrons of liberty, have dishonored the Christian name, and degraded human nature nearly to a level with the beasts that perish."[116]

The Baptist preacher, John Allen, was even more direct, and thundered,

> Blush ye pretended votaries of freedom! ye trifling Patriots! who are making a vain parade of being advocates for the liberties of mankind, who are thus

---

[114] Mark A. Knoll, *A History of Christianity in the United States and Canada* (Grand Rapids: Eerdmans, 1992), 109.

[115] Hart, 330.

[116] "How the American Revolution Shed Light on the Moral Problem of Slavery, *The Founding*, https://thefounding.net/the-american-revolution-shed-light-on-and-helped-to-abolish-slavery/; quoted Hart, 330.

making a mockery of your profession by trampling on the sacred natural rights and privileges of Africans.[117]

Opposition Increases

The opposition continued to increase. The anonymous author of *A Discourse on the Times* declared that if Americans would have the Lord on their side, "We must set at liberty those vast number of Africans, which have so long time been enslaved by us, who have as good a right to liberty as we have."[118]

David Avery, the chaplain who prayed over the Minutemen at The Battle of Bunker Hill (June 17, 1775), declared that if the states would begin the process of emancipating the slaves, it would be "a pleasing omen of the happy issue of our present struggle for liberty."[119]

Freeborn Garrettson (1752-1827), an evangelist from Maryland, freed his slaves after hearing God speak to him supernaturally. According to Garrettson, he heard the Lord say, "It is not right for you to keep your fellow creatures in bondage; you must let the oppressed go free." Garrettson immediately informed his slaves that they did not belong to him and that he did not desire their services without giving them proper compensation.

Garrettson began preaching against slavery and advocating for freedom, provoking intense opposition, especially in the

---

[117] John Coffey, *Exodus and Liberation* (Oxford: Oxford Univ. Press, 2014), 91; quoted in Hart, 330.

[118] *A Discourse on the Times* (Norwich, CT, 1776); quoted in Kidd, *God of Liberty*, 154.

[119] Kidd, *God of Liberty*, 154.

South. One enraged slave-owner came to the house where Garrettson was lodging and swore at him, threatened him, and punched him in the face. Garrettson did not retaliate but sought to reason with the man who finally gave up and left.

Garrettson took his message to North Carolina where he preached to slaves, seeking to "inculcate the doctrine of freedom in them."[120] His opposition to slavery was firmly rooted in the Gospel and he described a typical meeting with slaves, in which, he says, "Many of their sable faces were bedewed with tears, their withered hands of faith were stretched out, and their precious souls made white in the blood of the Lamb."[121]

Garrettson also preached to southern white audiences and sought to convince them of the evils of slavery and that God's will was liberty for all of His creatures. In Delaware, Garrettson visited Stokeley Sturgis' plantation and preached to both the slaves and the Sturgis family. He was able to convince Sturgis that slavery is a sin and Sturgis began making arrangements for his slaves to obtain freedom.

One of those who obtained his freedom was Richard Allen who became a successful evangelist to both black and white audiences. In 1784, he preached for several weeks in Radnor, Pennsylvania, to a mostly white audience, and he recalled hearing it said, "This man must

---

[120] Freeborn Garrettson, *The Experience and Travels of Mr. Freeborn Garretson* (Philadelphia, 1791).

[121] Garrettson, quoted in Kidd, *God of Liberty*, 160.

be a man of God; I have never heard such preaching before."[122] In 1787, he founded Bethel Methodist Church in Philadelphia out which emerged the African Methodist Episcopal (AME) denomination.

It was out of the Awakening that the American black church was born and became a positive force in American society, producing some of the nation's greatest preachers, singers, and musicians. The Civil Rights movement of the 1960s-1970s was anchored in the black churches of America and its most prominent leaders, such as Dr. Martin Luther King, Jr., (1929-1968) were ordained ministers—a legacy of 1726.

The Methodists

In 1744, John Wesley (1703–1791) spoke publicly against slavery, declaring that, in God's sight, blacks and whites are equal and that Christ died for all. Many Methodists in America, in both the North and South, picked up on Wesley's call and became some of the leading abolitionists in America.

James O'Kelly (1735-1826), for example, faced physical attacks because of his bold, excoriating preaching against slavery. He painted slaveholding as a debilitating and demonic kind of sin. It was, he said, "A work of the flesh, assisted by the devil; a mystery of iniquity, that works like witchcraft to darken your understanding, and harden your hearts against conviction."[123]

Because of the bold preaching of evangelists such as

---

[122] Richard Allen, *The Life, Experiences, and Gospel Labours of the Right Rev. Richard Allen* (Philadelphia, 1833), 5-8, 10, 16; quoted in Kidd, 197.

[123] Kidd, *God of Liberty*, 160.

Garrettson and O'Kelly, an anti-slavery movement gained momentum, even in the South. This movement faced intense opposition, as was the case in 1800 when Methodists in South Carolina circulated a petition calling for emancipation. A mob burned the handouts and dragged one of the Methodist preachers through the streets and almost drowned him in a well.

None of this slowed the momentum against slavery. In fact, the movement so permeated Methodism that a 1784 gathering of Methodist leaders in Baltimore denounced slavery as "contrary to the golden rule of God . . . and the unalienable rights of mankind, as well as every principle of the Revolution."[124]

They went a step further, requiring all members of Methodist churches, including those in the South, to begin emancipating their slaves. Those who refused to do so were to be expelled from the church. However, six months later, the demand was withdrawn because of the backlash in the South and due to allegations that the anti-slavery proponents were, in fact, British agents seeking to stir up a race war. Nonetheless, from this point forward, the South was on the defensive about the issue of slavery.

Proponents of slavery scrambled to devise moral arguments to justify the institution. A commonly held notion was that it was God's way of delivering Africans from paganism in their homeland, giving them an opportunity to hear the Gospel. Samuel Hopkins, however, dismantled this argument in his pamphlet entitled, *A Dialogue Concerning the Slavery of Africans:*

---

[124] Kidd, *God of Liberty*, 159.

Shewing It To Be the Duty and Interest of the American Colonies to Emancipate All the African Slaves.[125]

Although Hopkins would acknowledge God's providence in working out His plan—even through human acts of sin, as in the Old Testament story of Joseph—he systematically dismantled this argument as merely being an excuse for slavery. He thundered,

> What sort of "gospel" message is being conveyed when people are enslaved because of the color of their skin? The Declaration of Independence says all men are created equal with certain unalienable rights. Oh, the shocking, the intolerable inconsistencies![126]

The moral arguments against slavery were both obvious and compelling. These arguments were rooted in both Creation and Redemption. Creation tells us that all people are equal, with the genealogy of all humanity beginning with Adam and Eve. There is also equality in Redemption, for Christ died for all and His salvation is equally available to all who will believe. The old value systems that judged a person on the basis of race, gender, and social class were abolished in Christ (Galatians 3:27-28).

The Golden Rule was also used as an argument against slavery. David Barrow (1753–1819), a Baptist preacher from

---

[125] https://wisc.pb.unizin.org/ps601/chapter/samuel-hopkins-a-dialogue-concerning-the-slavery-of-the-africans/

[126] *A Dialogue Concerning the Slavery of Africans: Shewing It To Be the Duty and Interest of the American Colonies to Emancipate All the African Slaves,* https://digitalcollections.nypl.org/items/510d47e3-f853-a3d9-e040-e00a18064a99#/?uuid=510d47e3-f889-a3d9-e040-e00a18064a99

Virginia who became an abolitionist and freed his slaves, referred to "having a single eye to the Golden Rule" as the basis for emancipation. He insisted that if everyone practiced "Do to all men as you would they should do to you," it would soon put an end to slavery.

The Quakers

The Religious Society of Friends, commonly known as Quakers, were among the most ardent opponents of slavery in the New World. This is not surprising since one of their cardinal beliefs was the equality of all people before God, and so, they rejected the idea of hierarchy in both the church and society. The Friends arose in England in about 1650, and from the beginning, they lived out this belief in various ways. For example, they refused to show the expected honor to the upper classes by doffing their hats and by addressing them by their titles. This resulted in many of them being whipped and imprisoned, where hundreds died due to the filthy prison conditions.

It is not surprising, therefore, that when George Fox (1624-1691) visited the English colony of Barbados in 1671, he appealed to the Friends there to consider freeing their slaves. They should do this, he said, because not only are they equal by virtue of creation, but also because Christ died for all races.[127]

After Fox's visit, Quaker colonists in Barbados began questioning slavery and then denounced it openly in 1688. That same year, a joint meeting of Lutherans and Quakers in Germantown, Pennsylvania, issued a protest concerning

---

[127] Kidd, God of Liberty, 134.

the existence of slavery in the newly formed colony of Pennsylvania. Actually, as early as 1657, Fox had written a letter denouncing the captivity of Black and Indian slaves. The Quakers were actually the first to make a direct assault against slavery. Sixty years before the Emancipation Proclamation of January 1, 1863, there was not one Quaker slaveholder in America. They also participated in the mid-nineteenth century underground railroad that provided safe passage of escaped and freed slaves to the north.[128]

A Call for Action

Not all ministers, churches, and denominations embraced the Awakening and the abolition movement that accompanied it. Benjamin Rush (1745-1813), a Philadelphia physician, boldly confronted these timid custodians of the *status quo*. Rush was a member of the Continental Congress (1774–1781), as well as a signer of the Declaration of Independence. He also helped found the first American anti-slavery society. In the following address, he admonished the Christian ministers of America to take a bold stand against slavery. He wrote,

> But chiefly—ye ministers of the gospel, whose dominion over the principles and actions of men is so universally acknowledged and felt, - Ye who estimate the worth of your fellow creatures by their immortality, and therefore must look upon all mankind as equal; let your zeal keep pace with your opportunities to put a stop to slavery. While you enforce the duties of "tithe and cumin," neglect not

---

[128] Susan Hyatt, "The Good Fruit Remains," http://www.icwhp.org/quakers.html

the weightier laws of justice and humanity. Slavery is a Hydra sin and includes in it every violation of the precepts of the Laws and the Gospels. In vain will you command your flocks to offer up the incense of faith and charity, while they continue to mingle the sweat and blood of Negro slaves with their sacrifices. Remember, that national crimes require national punishments, and without declaring what punishment awaits this evil, you may venture to assure them, that it cannot pass with impunity, unless God shall cease to be just or merciful.[129]

The Founders Are Affected

The spiritual power of the Awakening and the moral arguments it produced against slavery were overwhelming. In fact, by the time of the writing of the Declaration of Independence in 1776 and the Constitution in 1787, virtually every Founder had taken a public stand against slavery. All agreed with John Adams, who stated the following:

> Every measure of prudence . . . ought to be assumed for the eventual total extirpation of slavery from the United States. I have throughout my whole life held the practice of slavery in abhorrence.[130]

However, deciding what to do with over two-million slaves who had not been versed in the responsibilities that would

---

[129] Benjamin Rush, "On Slavekeeping" (1773), found in William Bennett, *Our Sacred Honor* (New York: Simon and Schuster, 1997), 376-77.

[130] From John Adams to Robert J. Evans, 8 June 1819, https://founders.archives.gov/documents/Adams/99-02-02-7148

accompany freedom was another question. Sowell writes,

> Deciding that slavery was wrong was much easier than deciding what to do with millions of people from another continent, of another race, and without any historical preparation for living as free citizens in a society like that of the United States, where they were 20 percent of the population. It is clear from the private correspondence of Washington, Jefferson, and many others that their moral rejection of slavery was unambiguous, but the practical question of what to do now had them baffled. That would remain so for more than half a century.[131]

How to deal with the practicalities of freeing the slaves was especially challenging to the Founders from the South who had lived with slavery all of their lives. Some, like George Washington (1732-1799), freed their slaves; others lived with the contradiction of confessing that slavery was wrong, while continuing to own slaves out of long-held practice and convenience.

Patrick Henry (1736-1799), for example, spoke out passionately against slavery. This is clear in a letter to the Virginia Quaker, Robert Pleasants (1723–1801), who had sent Henry an anti-slavery tract, informing him that he had freed his slaves. In his response, Henry expressed complete agreement with Pleasants and said that slavery is "as repugnant to humanity, as it is inconsistent with the Bible and destructive of liberty." However, he then admitted his own sin, saying, "Would anyone believe I am the master of slaves of my own

---

[131] Sowell, "Twisted History,"
https://townhall.com/columnists/thomassowell/2003/12/17/twisted-history-n1057496

purchase! I am drawn along by the general inconvenience of living here without them."[132]

In contrast to Patrick Henry, two years before the Constitutional Convention, Benjamin Franklin liberated his two slaves and began advocating for abolition. George Washington's situation was more complex. He had inherited a large plantation with a large number of slaves, and he realized that to thrust them suddenly and unprepared out into the world would have been unwise, and perhaps, harmful to them.

To remedy the situation, Washington set up a compassionate program to disentangle Mt. Vernon from the institution of slavery. Those slaves who wanted to leave were free to do so. Those who chose to remain were paid wages, and he began a program to educate and prepare the children of slaves for freedom. He declared,

> I clearly foresee that nothing but the rooting out of slavery can perpetuate the existence of our union by consolidating it in a common bond of principle.[133]

The Power of Revitalized Christianity

This is a fact: It was a revitalized Christianity that provided the spiritual and moral forces that would eventually bring an end to slavery in America. It was the Great Awakening that produced the unique moral outrage, of which Drs. Sowell and Williams speak. 1726, the year the Awakening began, was a defining moment in America's history.

---

[132] Kidd, God of Liberty, 147.

[133] John Bernard, *Retrospections of America, 1797–1811*, 91 (1887); quoted by Hart, 332.

Although it would take a Second Great Awakening *(ca.* 1800- *ca.* 1830), a Great Prayer Awakening (1857-58), and a Civil War (1861-1865) to bring final closure, slavery's end was sealed in that First Great Awakening that swept Colonial America. 1726 marked the beginning of the end of slavery in America.

We ought, therefore, to take a lesson from history and pray for another Great Awakening to sweep across the land. We should recall the words of Samuel Adams (1722–1803), who served as Governor of Massachusetts (1793- 1797) and who was known as *The Father of the American Revolution.* On February 28, 1795, he declared April 2, 1795 as a Day of Fasting and Prayer for both Massachusetts and America. The words of that Proclamation reveal the profound depth of Christian faith in America's founding generation. In part, it reads as follows:

> The Supreme Ruler of the Universe, having been pleased, in the course of His Providence, to establish the independence of the United States of America . . . I have therefore thought fit to appoint, and with the advice and consent of the Council, I do hereby appoint Thursday, the Second Day of April next, to be observed as a Day of Public Fasting, Humiliation and Prayer throughout this Commonwealth: Calling upon the Ministers of the Gospel, of every Denomination, with their respective Congregations, to assemble on that Day, and devoutly implore the Divine forgiveness of our Sins, To pray that the Light of the Gospel, and the rights of Conscience, may be continued to the people of United America; and that his Holy Word may be improved by them, so that the name of God may be exalted, and their own Liberty and Happiness secured.

Chapter 9

A Nation Emerges From The Awakening

> The Declaration of Independence of 1776 was a result of the evangelical preaching of the evangelists of the Great Awakening.
>
> *Perry Miller (1905-1963), Harvard Professor*

The Great Awakening's influence on the First Continental Congress was obvious. This strategic gathering met for the first time at Carpenter's Hall in Philadelphia on September 5, 1774. The first session opened with an extended time of Bible reading and prayer, and prayer continued to be a vital part of each day's proceedings.

The main purpose of the Congress was to formulate a unified response to British oppression. This was necessary because, at the same time that the colonists were experiencing spiritual awakening, Britain was imposing oppressive taxes and regulations on them without their input. Perhaps, it was like the tongue-in-cheek remark: When God opens the windows of heaven, the devil opens the door of hell, and you are caught in between.

King George III obviously looked upon the colonists as

subjects rather than as citizens, as well as a source of revenue for the British Crown. Government acts such as The Sugar Act (1764), the Stamp Act (1765), the Townshend Act (1767), and others, imposed taxes and tariffs, which led to fervent protests throughout the Colonies, and especially in New England. *No Taxation without Representation* became a common cry.

The Colonists also resented the fact that the British Crown had begun sending governors who set up customs offices in the colonies to oversee its interests and to enforce regulations and the collection of taxes. With emotions running high, violence erupted at times. Most famous of these was the Boston Massacre that occurred on March 5, 1770, when British soldiers fired into a crowd of protestors, killing five Boston citizens.

One of the fallen was Crispus Attucks (1723-1770), a black man of African and Native American lineage. A former slave who had obtained his freedom and settled in Boston, Attucks was a leader in the protests against British oppression. Years later, in 1888, a monument was erected in memory of those who had fallen that day. On that occasion, a poem was recited honoring him. It described him as

Leader and voice that day;
The first to defy, and the first to die.[134]

The Situation Becomes Intolerable

With such protests flaring up, especially in New England, King George III and Parliament decided to teach the upstart

---

[134] T. Harry Williams, Richard N. Current and Frank Freidel, *A History of the United States to 1877* (New York: Random House, 1959), 132.

colonists a lesson by imposing a series of laws that became known as *The Intolerable Acts* (1774). These Acts closed the Boston seaport to all shipping and revoked the right of the people of Massachusetts to self-governance, something they had known since the days of the Pilgrims and Winthrop. Furthermore, instead of officials being elected by the people, they were now to be appointed by the British Crown. Six regiments of British soldiers were assigned to occupy Boston to enforce these measures.

Throughout the Colonies, from north to south, residents identified with the people of Boston in their distress, and special days of prayer and fasting were held. In Virginia, for example, a resolution drafted by Thomas Jefferson was approved, making June 1 a day of fasting and prayer, and asking that all the oppressed people of America would, "Invoke the divine interposition to give the American people one heart and one mind to oppose all transgressions against American rights."[135]

The First Continental Congress Opens with Prayer

In Philadelphia in 1774, delegates gathered to formulate a strategy against oppressive British control. This gathering, known as the First Continental Congress, had representatives from all of the Colonies except Georgia. As they were about to begin, it was suggested that they open with prayer. Two delegates opposed the motion, however, on the grounds that they, being such a diverse group consisting of Anglicans,

---

[135] *Watchmen on the Wall*, https://www.frc.org/prayerteam/prayer-targets-fasting-humiliation-and-prayer-made-america-scandal-the-urgent-call2fall; Also quoted by Hart, 260.

Quakers, Presbyterians, and Puritans, would not be able to pray together. At this point, Samuel Adams, a Puritan from Boston who had been affected favorably by the Awakening, stood and said that he was not a bigoted man and that he could join in prayer with any person of piety and virtue who loved his country. He went on to say that, although he was a stranger in Philadelphia, he had heard of an Anglican minister, a Reverend Jacob Duché (1739-1798), who was such a man, and he proposed that they invite him to lead them in prayer. Adams' proposal was approved and Duché was asked to preside over a time of Bible reading and prayer.

As the elderly, grey-haired Duché stood before the Congress, he began by reading Psalm 35, in its entirety. A prayer of David for deliverance, it had a powerful impact on everyone present. It begins with the words, *Plead my cause, O, LORD, with those who strive with me; Fight against those who fight against me.* The Psalm ends with praise for God's deliverance.

As the Psalm was read, a unique sense of God's presence filled the room and tears flowed from many eyes. John Adams wrote to his wife, Abigail, sharing with her the impact of the Bible reading and prayer on the delegates.

> Who can realize the emotions with which they turned imploringly to heaven for divine interposition and aid. It was enough to melt a heart of stone. I never saw a greater effect upon an audience. It seems as if heaven had ordained that Psalm to be read that day. I saw tears gush into the eyes of the old, grave pacific Quakers of Philadelphia. I must beg you to read that Psalm.[136]

---

[136] William Hunt, *American Biographical Panorama* (Albany: Joel Musnell, 1849), 46; quoted in Federer, 137.

Following his reading of the Psalm, Duché began praying for the delegates, for America, and especially for the city of Boston and its inhabitants who were under siege. As he began praying, the Anglicans, such as George Washington and Richard Henry Lee, knelt in prayer, according to their custom. The Puritans, according to their custom, sat with bowed heads, and prayed. Others prayed in the manner unique to them. Despite the differences, a singleness of heart and purpose prevailed as they united in prayer for God's assistance and intervention for America.

Prayer continued to be a vital part of the daily proceedings of the Continental Congresses. Indeed, the Roman Catholic scholar, Michael Novak, is correct in saying, "In all moments of imminent danger, as in the first Act of the First Continental Congress, the founding generation turned to prayer."[137]

The Declaration of Independence

With the British tightening the screws of control, and after much prayer and discussion, the delegates of the Continental Congress decided that the time had come to declare their independence. Thomas Jefferson (1743–1826) was chosen to draft the document, and a select committee of five, including Benjamin Franklin, was chosen to assist in its creation. On July 4, 1776, it was read publicly for the first time.

This founding document anchors individual rights, not in any human institution or government, but in God.

> *We hold these truths to be self-evident that all men [people] are created equal and are endowed by their Creator with certain inalienable rights such as life, liberty and the pursuit of happiness.*

---

[137] Novak, 18.

Jefferson, Franklin, and the other Founders understood human rights to have a transcendent source, that being, God Himself. These men and their forebears had suffered the loss of their rights. They knew what it was like for those rights to be given and taken at the whim of a monarch, pope, or bishop. In this new nation, therefore, they were determined to put the rights of the individual in a place legally beyond human reach. Government, they insisted, did not exist to give or take rights, but instead, to protect those rights already given by God.

References to God in the Declaration

Three names for God used in the Declaration are drawn directly from the Judeo-Christian tradition. They are *Creator, Supreme Judge,* and *Divine Providence.* They did not use Christian, redemptive words in the document, such as *Savior* or *Redeemer,* for they were aware that they were formulating, not a statement of faith for a church, but the founding document for a nation.

The appeal to the laws of nature and *Nature's God* has been commonly considered an ambiguous reference to deity rooted in the Enlightenment (1715–1789). That is not necessarily true, for even a fiery, evangelical revivalist like Whitefield was known to use the term, *Nature's God.* He did so, for example, in a sermon describing the earthquake and the darkening of the sun at the time of Christ's death, declaring, "See how all nature is in agony . . . as it were to see the God of nature suffer."[138]

---

[138] George Whitefield, *Sermons of George Whitefield* (Peabody, MA: Hendrickson, 2009), 110.

Considering Franklin's close friendship with Whitefield, as well as the fact that he was a member of the committee formulating the Declaration, it is not implausible to acknowledge the influence of the Awakening in the expression, *Nature's God*. Franklin, after all, not only heard Whitefield preach many times, but he also printed and distributed many of his sermons.

The use of these names for God confirms what is expressed in so many ways by the Founders; that is, they considered belief in God as Creator and Judge to be essential for good citizenship. Unless the citizens were to have a moral sense of obligation to their Creator, they would tend to live self-centered lives that would be harmful to society at large. This is why James Madison (1751–1836) wrote,

> The belief in a God All Powerful, wise and good, is so essential to the moral order of the world and to the happiness of man, that arguments which enforce it cannot be drawn from too many sources nor adapted with too much solicitude to the different characters and capacities impressed with it.[139]

The use of the word *Providence* is especially interesting, for it was commonly used as a synonym for the God of the Bible in the 18th Century, even by ministers. It was not, as some have suggested, a generic, impersonal reference to deity. Even a fiery revivalist such as Whitefield often used it in referring to God.

Providence is a word that expresses faith in God as the One who is superintending the course of history and who is

---

[139] Letter from James Madison to Frederick Beasley, 20 November 1825, https://founders.archives.gov/documents/Madison/04-03-02-0663.

overruling, even the actions of evil men, in order to bring about His plan and purpose. This is why Roger Williams (1603–1683), after being banished from Massachusetts by the Puritans in 1636, and making his way in the winter to Rhode Island, founded a city there, which he named *Providence*. This expressed his faith that God would overrule the wrong that he believed had been done to him and would bring about His plan for his life.

John Witherspoon (1723–1794), a member of the Continental Congress, preached a sermon entitled *The Dominion of Providence over the Passions of Men,* less than two months before signing the Declaration. Witherspoon, a Presbyterian minister was President of the College of New Jersey, which is now Princeton University. In this 1776 sermon on *Providence,* he emphasized the necessity of believing that God would bring good out of the evil situation of the day; that is, that the ambition of mistaken princes and the cruelty of oppressive rulers would finally promote the glory of God.[140] This is *Providence.*

The final paragraph of the Declaration shows that this was the faith of the Founders, for in it, they express their trust in God for His providential protection and support in their momentous act. It reads:

> And for the support of this declaration, with a firm reliance on the protection of Divine Providence, we mutually pledge to each other our Lives, our Fortunes, and our sacred Honor.

After the signing of the document, and knowing that King

---

[140] John Witherspoon, "Dominion of Providence Over the Passions of Men," 1776, https://oll.libertyfund.org/pages/1776-witherspoon-dominion-of-providence-over-the-passions-of-men-sermon.

George III would view their actions as treason, John Hancock exhorted, "We must all hang together." Franklin is said to have quipped, "Yes, we must hang together, or, most assuredly, we will all hang separately."

After the Declaration was published, Jacob Duché, who had become the chaplain for the Congress, prayed the following prayer and it was recorded in the proceedings of the Congress. He prayed,

> O Lord, our high and mighty Father, heavenly king of kings, and Lord of Lords, who dost from Thy throne behold all the dwellers of the earth, and reignest with power supreme over all kingdoms, empires, and governments. Look down in mercy we beseech thee on these our American states who have fled to Thee from the rod of the oppressor and thrown themselves on Thy gracious protection, desiring to be henceforth dependent only on Thee. To Thee they have appealed for the righteousness of their cause; to Thee do they now look up for that countenance and support which Thou alone can give . . . Shower down upon them and the millions they represent, such temporal blessings as Thou seest expedient for them in this world and crown them with everlasting joy in the world to come. All this we ask in the name and through the merits of Jesus Christ Thy Son and our Saviour. Amen.[141]

A Praying Colonial Army

The signing of the Declaration was the final straw for King

---

[141] J.L. Forwood, "Dr. Jackson and His Class," vol. 1 of *Proceedings of the Delaware County Historical Society* (Chester, PA, 1902), 14.

George III, who did consider their action to be an act of treason. He, therefore, made plans to put down the "rebellion" in the Colonies by force and he began sending British war ships and additional troops to America's shores.

The Continental Congress was prepared. On May 10, 1775, they had asked George Washington to become commander-in-chief of the ragtag Colonial militias and to transform them into an army that could face the mighty British war machine. Washington accepted the call and immediately began to instill in the Colonial troops a very real faith in God. Novak says,

> Washington knew his only hope lay in a profound conviction in the hearts and daily actions of all his men that what they did they did for God, and under God's protection.[142]

Washington, therefore, issued an order stating that each day was to begin with prayer led by the officers of each unit. He also ordered that, unless their duties required them to be elsewhere, every soldier was to observe "a punctual attendance of Divine services, to implore the blessing of heaven upon the means used for our safety and public defense."[143] He also forbade profanity, swearing, gambling and drunkenness and expressed his desire that, "Every officer and man will endeavor so as to live and act as becomes a Christian soldier."[144]

At one point, during a particularly difficult part of the war, Washington and his men were quartering at Valley Forge.

---

[142] Novak, 19.

[143] Federer, 638.

[144] Federer, 639.

Rev. Henry Muhlenberg (1711–1787), pastor of a nearby Lutheran Church observed Washington's activities. He wrote, "Washington rode around among his army yesterday and admonished each one to fear God."[145] Muhlenberg went on to say,

> This gentleman does not belong to the so-called world of society, for he respects God's word, believes in atonement through Christ, and bears himself in humility and gentleness. It appears that the Lord God has singularly, yea marvelously, preserved him from harm in the midst of countless perils . . . and hath hitherto graciously held him in His hand as His chosen vessel.[146]

That Washington was a devout Christian in his private life was confirmed by Isaac Potts (1750 – 1803), a Quaker who lived near Valley Forge where the Continental Army, under Washington's command, was wintering. One day, during this—one of the bleakest periods of the war—Potts was riding through the woods when he came upon Washington during a time of private prayer. For Potts, this was a life-changing experience. As a Quaker, he was a pacifist, but his encounter of Washington in prayer caused him to rethink his view. He said,

> I heard a plaintive sound as of a man at prayer. I tied my horse to a sapling and went quietly into the woods and to my astonishment I saw the great George Washington on his knees alone, with his sword on one side and his cocked hat on the other. He was at Prayer to the God of the Armies, beseeching to

---

[145] Hart, 293.
[146] Hart, 293.

interpose with his Divine aid, as it was ye Crisis, and the cause of the country, of humanity and of the world. Such a prayer I never heard from the lips of man. I left him alone praying. I went home and told my wife I saw a sight and heard today what I never saw or heard before, and just related to her what I had seen and heard and observed. We never thought a man could be a soldier and a Christian, but if there is one in the world, it is Washington.[147]

The Congress and the Nation Pray

During the Revolutionary War (April 19, 1775–September 3, 1783), the Congress issued no fewer than fifteen separate calls for special days of prayer and fasting. For example, during the fall of 1776, when the morale of the army and populace had sunk to an all-time low because of a poor harvest and hardship on the battlefield, Congress proclaimed December 11, 1776, as a Day of Fasting and Repentance.

John Witherspoon, the Protestant Reformer and member of the Congress, was deputized to write the proclamation, which was then approved by the rest of the Congress. It reads, in part,

WHEREAS, the war in which the United States are engaged with Great Britain, has not only been prolonged, but is likely to be carried to the greatest extremity; and whence it becomes all public bodies, as well as private persons, to reverence the Providence of God, and look up to him as the supreme disposer

---

[147] Arnold Friberg, "The Prayer at Valley Forge," http://www. revolutionary-war-and-beyond.com/prayer-at-valley-forge.html

of all events, and the arbiter of the fate of nations; therefore; RESOLVED, That it be recommended to all the United States, as soon as possible, to appoint a day of solemn fasting and humiliation; to implore of Almighty God the forgiveness of the many sins prevailing among all ranks, and to beg the assistance of his Providence in the prosecution of the present just and necessary war. The Congress do also, in the most earnest manner, recommend to the members of the United States, and particularly the officers civil and military under them, the exercise of repentance and reformation, and the strict observance of the articles of war, particularly that part which forbids profane swearing and all immorality, of which all such officers are desired to take notice.[148]

Indeed, there was an amazing change in circumstances after this day of prayer, including successes on the battlefield and the reaping of abundant harvests. There was, in fact, such a turnaround after this that Congress issued proclamations for national Days of Thanksgiving on October 20, 1779, October 26, 1781, and October 11, 1782. They encouraged the people of America to set aside those days as special days of thanksgiving because, "It hath pleased Almighty God, the father of mercies, remarkably to assist and support the United States of America in their important struggle for liberty."[149]

Novak says that a sampling of the words set forth in this

---

[148] "Fast Day Proclamation of the Continental Congress, December 11, 1776," Washington C. Ford, Gaillard Hunt, eds., vol. 6, *The Journals of the Continental Congress, 1777-1789* (Washington, D.C.: Government Printing Office, 1904-37), 1022.

[149] Novak, 22.

and other Proclamations of Prayer and Thanksgiving, "testifies to the covenant the people had entered into with the God of liberty." He goes on to say that the Founders, like the first immigrants to this land, had a sense of Divine purpose, and that is why, "Later on, Lincoln called Americans 'an almost chosen people,' just as many before him had seen our nation as a 'second Israel.'"[150]

Independence Achieved

The Revolutionary War lasted a total of seven years, with the major American victory at Yorktown, VA in 1781 marking the end of hostilities. The Treaty of Paris was signed two years later, in 1783, thus officially ending the conflict. It was a costly war, especially for the signers of the Declaration of Independence.

Indeed, all 56 were targeted by the British. Nine died of wounds or hardships during the war. Five were captured and imprisoned, in each case, enduring brutal treatment. Several lost wives, sons, or entire families. One lost his thirteen children. Two wives were brutally treated. All were, at one time or another, the victims of manhunts and were driven from their homes. Twelve signers had their homes completely burned. Seventeen lost everything they owned. Yet not one defected or went back on his pledged word.[151]

The war officially came to an end on October 19, 1781, when the British General, Cornwallis, surrendered his entire force to Washington. In customary fashion, Cornwallis turned his sword over to Washington, and the weaponry of his troops was stacked in neat piles. According to historian, Benjamin

---

[150] Novak, 23.

[151] Novak, 157-58.

Hart, as this was happening, the British corps played, "The World Turned Upside Down."[152] For the Americans, however, the world had been turned right side up.

Washington then appointed Israel Evans, a chaplain in the Revolutionary army, to deliver a thanksgiving sermon to the troops that same day. According to Thomas S. Kidd, Professor of History at Baylor University, Evans may have addressed the largest assembly gathered in America since George Whitefield's massive evangelistic meetings in the 1740s.[153]

In his sermon, and in a poem appended to the published version, Evans exhorted the troops to give thanks to God, knowing that their victory over the British was not the result of their own strength and prowess. His poem also shows how the founding generation identified with Israel of the Old Testament and believed that the same God that fought for Israel had fought for them.

To Him who led in ancient days,
The Hebrew tribes, your anthems raise;
The God who spoke from Sinai's hill,
Protects His chosen people still.
Not in ourselves success we owe,
By help divine we crushed the foe,
In sword and shield who vainly trust,
Shall soon be humbled in the dust.
Praise Him who gives us to repel,
The powers of Britain and of hell.
With thankful hearts his goodness own,
And bow before Jehovah's throne.[154]

---

[152] Hart, 298.
[153] Kidd, *God of Liberty*, 127.
[154] Kidd, *God of Liberty*, 127.

At this point, having completed his commission, Washington issued a letter of resignation as Commander-In-Chief to the Continental Congress. He then wrote what could be described as a pastoral letter, dated June 14, 1783, to the governors of the various states. This letter included his "earnest prayer" that is here quoted in part. He wrote,

> I now make it my earnest prayer that God would have you, and the State over which you preside, in his holy protection; that he would incline the hearts of the citizens . . . to entertain a brotherly affection and love for one another . . . and to demean ourselves with that charity, humility, and pacific temper of mind, which were the characteristics of the Divine Author of our blessed religion, and without a humble imitation of His example in these things, we can never hope to be a happy nation.[155]

Our Response

Seeing the vital role of faith and prayer in the birthing of this nation, let us not be intimidated by the assertion that prayer is somehow inappropriate for public or political venues. Let us be bold in our faith. Let us be salt and light in this generation. Let us pray. It is the godly thing to do! It is the American thing to do!

---

[155] Novak, 20.

Chapter 10

America's Colorblind Founding Documents

> I have a dream that one day this nation will rise up
> and live out the true meaning of its creed:
> "We hold these truths to be self-evident,
> that all men are created equal.".
>
> *Dr. Martin Luther King, Jr. (1929-1968)*

Had foreign visitors read America's founding documents at the time of their enactment, they would not have known that slavery existed in America. No mention is made of slaves or slavery. There is no reference to individuals on the basis of race, ethnicity, or skin color. Instead of using race classifications, the Constitution speaks of "citizens," "persons," and "other persons."

Nothing in either the Declaration of Independence or the United States Constitution indicates that the freedoms guaranteed do not apply to every individual. Dr. Martin Luther King, Jr. (1929–1968) understood this, and in his stirring, *I Have a Dream* speech, he challenged America, not to dispense with its founding documents, but instead, to live up to them. Quoting from the Declaration, he declared his hope:

That one day this nation will rise up and live out the true meaning of its creed: "We hold these truths to be self-evident, that all men are created equal."

 Showing that he understood these freedoms to be rooted in the country's Christian origins, Dr. King, who was himself a devout Christian, went on to say that he had a dream that one day all Americans, whether white or black, would be able to sing together the words of that Christian, patriotic hymn,

My country 'tis of Thee,
Sweet land of liberty, of Thee I sing.
Land where my fathers died,
Land of the Pilgrim's pride,
From every mountainside,
Let freedom ring!

Thanks to 1726, America's founding documents are colorblind, even if her history has not been. The famous abolitionist, Frederick Douglass (1818–1895), understood this and argued that the language of the founding documents must be understood as applying to everyone. "Any one of these provisions in the hands of abolition statesmen, and backed by a right moral sentiment," he declared, "would put an end to slavery in America."[156]

This absence of any mention of slavery in the Constitution

---

[156] David Azerrad, "What the Constitution Really Says about Race and Slavery," The Heritage Foundation, https://www.heritage.org/the-constitution/commentary/what-the-constitution-really-says-about-race-and-slavery.

was purposeful, for James Madison said, "The Convention thought it wrong to admit in the Constitution the idea that there could be property in men."[157]

This shows that the Founders grappled with how to bring the southern states into the Union without affirming slavery. They knew that if the southern states were not included in the Union, they would align with the British or other European powers and be a constant thorn in the side of the new nation. How to include them without affirming slavery was the challenge.

In the end, concessions were made at the Convention in order to bring in all thirteen colonies. Dr. Sowell has said,

> But don't pretend that it was an easy answer—or that those who grappled with the dilemma in the 18th century were some special villains when most leaders and most people around the world saw nothing wrong with slavery.[158]

The Three-Fifths Clause

One of the most misunderstood sections of the Constitution is the so-called *three-fifths clause* in which only three-fifths of the slave population of southern states would be counted for representation. This had nothing to do with assigning value based on race, as many have alleged. Instead, it was

---

[157] Walter E. Williams, "Slavery is Neither Peculiar or Strange," https://www.creators.com/read/walter-williams/05/19/slavery-is-neither-strange-nor-peculiar.

[158] Thomas Sowell, "Twisted History," https://townhall.com/columnists/thomassowell/2003/12/17/twisted-history-n1057496.

related to keeping the southern states from gaining too much power in the new Congress where the number of representatives from each state would be tied to the population of that state.

The southern states wanted to include their slave populations in the census in order to gain the most possible representatives and as much power as possible, even though they did not allow slaves to vote. The three-fifths compromise was a way of diminishing the influence of the South in the new Congress in that it counted only three-fifths of the slave population for purposes of representation.

Even here, the Founders did not use the word "slaves" or "slavery," but instead, used the term "other persons." Abraham Lincoln (1809–1865) described this refusal of the Founders to acknowledge slavery in the Constitution as being like a man who hides an ugly, cancerous growth until the time comes that it can be eradicated from his body.

That the three-fifths clause was not about assigning value based on race is confirmed by the fact that, at the time of the Constitutional Convention, there were at least 60,000 free blacks in northern and southern states who were counted the same as whites when it came to determining the number of representatives to Congress. Additionally, it is important to note that there were as many as ten states where blacks had full voting privileges.[159]

Moral Outrage
at the Constitutional Convention

---

[159] Azerrad, "What the Constitution Really Says About Race and Slavery," https://www.heritage.org/the-constitution/commentary/what-the-constitution-really-says-about-race-and-slavery.

At the Constitutional Convention concessions were made toward the southern states to bring them into the Union. Many, however, were not happy with these concessions. For example, Virginian, George Mason (1725-1792), argued for the immediate outlawing of slavery. Warning of God's judgement, if they allowed slavery to continue, he said,

> Every master is born a petty tyrant. They bring the judgment of Heaven upon a country. As nations cannot be rewarded or punished in the next world, they must be in this. By an inevitable chain of causes and effects, Providence punishes national sins by national calamities.[160]

Many see the Civil War, with the loss of 700,000 lives, as the judgment predicted by Mason. Thomas Jefferson shared Mason's concern, for it was in the context of the continued existence of slavery, that he wrote:

> God who gave us life, gave us liberty. And can the liberties of a nation be thought secure when we have removed their only firm basis, a conviction in the minds of the people that these liberties are a gift from God? That they are not to be violated but with His wrath? Indeed, I tremble for my country when I reflect that God is just and that His justice cannot sleep forever.[161]

---

[160] Jonathan Eliot, ed., *The Debates in the Several State Constitutions on the Adoption of the Federal Constitution as Recommended by the General Convention at Philadelphia in 1787* (Philadelphia: J.B. Lippincott Co., 1836), 458.

[161] Thomas Jefferson, "Notes on the State of Virginia, Query XVIII: Manners, Thomas Jefferson/1781," https://teachingamericanhistory.org/library/document/notes-on-the-state-of-virginia-query-xviii-manners/

The Founders
Dealt Slavery a Mortal Blow

With this sort of Biblical and moral opposition to slavery at the time of the nation's founding, it is easy to see how slavery's days were already numbered. This moral outrage would flower into the Abolition Movement of the next century (1830s-1870), and finally would lead to the abolishment of slavery after a Great Prayer Awakening (1856-1857) and Civil War (1861-1865).[162]

Demonstrating that they were serious about abolishing slavery, the Founders outlawed slavery in the newly formed Northwest Territory. They also worded the Constitution in such a way that the rights guaranteed therein could not be denied to anyone based on race or skin color. In formulating the founding documents, the Founders dealt slavery a mortal blow, from which it would not recover.

They Saw the Hand of God

The task of formulating a Constitution that would gain the support of all 13 colonies was truly a herculean task. At one point, the Convention was on the verge of disbanding due to unresolved regional disputes. It was at this point that Benjamin Franklin called the delegates to prayer, quoting Psalm 127:1, *Unless the LORD builds the house, they labor in vain who build it.*

It is an indisputable fact that 1726 is indelibly stamped on America's founding documents. Indeed, there was a consensus

---

[162] In my book, *The Great Prayer Awakening of 1857-58*, I document the great prayer movement that helped end slavery once and for all.

among the Founders that America had come forth providentially by the Hand of God. Reflecting on the completed work of the Constitutional Convention, James Madison (1751–1836), the chief architect of the Constitution, declared,

> It is impossible for the man of pious reflection not to perceive in it a finger of that Almighty hand which has been so frequently and signally extended to our relief in critical stages of the Revolution.[163]

Benjamin Rush, the physician from Philadelphia who signed the Declaration of Independence and led the state of Pennsylvania in ratifying the Constitution, was even more blunt in his belief that God had influenced the formulation of the Constitution. He declared that he ". . . as much believed the hand of God was employed in this work as that God had divided the Red Sea to give a passage to the children of Israel or had fulminated the Ten Commandments from Mount Sinai."[164]

America Is Not Racist

Many secularists insist that America was founded on racist principles. They are wrong. David Azerrad was correct when he said, "The argument that the Constitution is racist suffers from one fatal flaw: the concept of race does not exist in the Constitution."[165] There are racists in America, but

---

[163] *The Federalist Papers*, No. 37 (11 Jan. 1788), New York: Mentor Books, 1961), 230-31.

[164] W. Cleon Skousen, *The 5000 Year Leap* (USA: National Center for Constitutional Studies, 1991), vi.

[165] David Azerrad, "What the Constitution Really Says About Race and Slavery," *The Daily Signal*, December 28, 2015, 1.

America itself is not racist. America's founding documents are colorblind.

The Founders did not invent slavery. They were born into a world where slavery already existed and was accepted all over the world. They were not perfect, and it can be argued that they conceded too much at the time. Nonetheless, they did an admirable job of formulating founding documents that would eventually eradicate that horrendous institution and make America *the land of the free and home of the brave,* with people of every race and ethnicity wanting to live here.

Chapter 11

The Faith of
The Founders

The general principles on which the fathers achieved
independence were . . . the general principles of Christianity.
Now I will avow that I then believed, and now believe,
that those general principles of Christianity are as eternal and
immutable as the existence and attributes of God.

John Adams (1735-1826)

There is no question that most—if not all—of the Founding Fathers were influenced, to one degree or another, by the Great Awakening. For example, Benjamin Rush (1746-1813), one of the signers of the Declaration of Independence and a central figure at the Continental Congress, attributed the development of his thinking and ideals to the preachers of the Great Awakening.[166] In their excellent book, *Never Before in History: America's Inspired Birth*, Amos and Gardiner write,

> The majority of people who founded the United States
> of America either experienced, or were children of

---

[166] Benjamin Rush, *Autobiography of Benjamin Rush*, G.W. Corner, ed. (Princeton: Princeton Univ. Press, 1948), 23-37.

those who experienced, the religious awakening of the 1740s.[167]

This meant that their Christianity, for the most part, was not a dry, formal orthodoxy based on church membership, but was, instead, a vital faith that was both known in the head and experienced in the heart. Their Christianity was not one of externals, characterized by such things as church membership, church attendance, priests, vestments, rituals, and the like. Instead, their Christianity was internal—of the heart—and something to be expressed in daily life. In other words, it was more lifestyle than religious ritual.

A cursory examination of the writings, speeches, and actions of the Founding Fathers is enough to establish their commitment to Christian principles. Prayers and Bible readings, along with other expressions of faith in God, the Bible, and Jesus Christ permeate their writings.

I am here presenting four of the best-known Founders; George Washington, Benjamin Franklin, James Madison, and Thomas Jefferson; and three lesser-known Founders, John Witherspoon, Benjamin Rush, and John Carroll. Exhibited in their writings and character is a common respect and commitment to Christian principles and values.

George Washington

George Washington (1732–1799) was born in Westmoreland County, Virginia, to Augustine Washington and his wife, Mary Ball Washington. When George was 11 years old, his father died, creating a situation in which he had to develop a sense of responsibility at a very young age.

---

[167] Gary Amos and Richard Gardiner, 56.

Washington's mother was a devout Christian who sought to raise him to be a truly committed believer in Christ. When he was leaving home as a young soldier, she told him: "Remember that God is our only sure trust." She reminded him: "My son, neglect not the duty of secret prayer."[168]

Washington's mother was, no doubt, influenced by the Great Awakening, for it had a profound impact on the state of Virginia. This was confirmed by Charles Hodge, who in a pamphlet written in 1839 and entitled, "The Constitutional History of the Presbyterian Church in the United States of America," says, "In no part of our country was the revival more interesting, and in very few was it so pure as in Virginia." [169] Both her faith and the faith of her son were characteristic of those impacted by the Great Awakening. This was made startlingly clear in a prayer journal kept by Washington when he was in his twenties.

In April of 1891, several of Washington's descendants, including Lawrence Washington, Bushrod Washington, and Thomas B. Washington, sold a collection of his personal items at auction in Philadelphia.

---

[168] William J. Johnson, *George Washington the Christian* (New York: Abingdon, 1919), 36.

[169] Charles Hodge, "The Constitutional History of the Presbyterian Church in the United State," *The Christian History of the American Revolution,* Verna M. Hall, ed. (San Francisco: The Foundation for American Christian Education, 1975), 123.

Among the items was a little book filled with daily prayers in Washington's handwriting when he was in his twenties. Entitled, *Daily Sacrifice,* these prayers are deeply devotional and evangelical in nature. For example, the first entry reads, in part,

> Let my heart, therefore, gracious God, be so affected with the glory and majesty of Thine honor that I may not do my own works, but wait on Thee, and discharge those duties which Thou requirest of me.[170]

The following Monday morning, his prayer reads,

> Direct my thoughts, words and work, wash away my sins in the immaculate blood of the Lamb, and purge my heart by Thy Holy Spirit . . . daily frame me more and more in the likeness of Thy Son Jesus Christ.[171]

Also, of note is his prayer:

> Bless, O Lord, the whole race of mankind, and let the world be filled with the knowledge of Thee and Thy Son, Jesus Christ.[172]

Commenting on this prayer book, Professor S. F. Upham, of Drew Theological Seminary, wrote,

> The "Daily Prayers" of George Washington abound in earnest thought, expressed in simple, beautiful, fervent and evangelical language. They reveal to us the real life of the great patriot, and attest his piety. None can read these petitions, which bore his desires

---

[170] Johnson, *George Washington the Christian*, 24.

[171] Johnson, 27.

[172] William J. Johnson, *George Washington, the Christian* (New York: Abingdon Press, 1919), 24-35.

to God, and often brought answers of peace, without having a grander conception of Washington's character. The prayers are characterized by a deep consciousness of sin and by a need for forgiveness, and by a recognition of dependence upon the merits and mercies of our Lord [173]

Washington insisted on taking the oath of office with his hand placed on a Bible. By connecting the presidential oath with the Holy Scriptures, Washington made clear that he saw this act as a sacred oath before God. Indeed, historian Benjamin Hart notes,

> The U.S. Constitution has worked because there has been a sacred aura surrounding the document; it has been something more than a legal contract; it was a covenant, an oath before God, very much related to the covenant the Pilgrims signed. Indeed, when the President takes his oath of office, he places his hand on a Bible and swears before Almighty God to uphold the Constitution of the United States. He makes a sacred promise; and the same holds true for Supreme Court justices who take an oath to follow the letter of the written Constitution. The moment America's leaders begin treating the Constitution as though it were a mere sheet of paper is the moment the American Republic—or American Covenant— ends.[174]

Washington delivered his first inaugural address on April 30, 1789. It was filled with references to God and the Bible. At the close of the ceremony in New York City, he and

---

[173] Johnson, 24.
[174] Hart, 77.

Congress proceeded to St. Paul's Chapel where they participated in a worship service.[175]

Washington's deep faith was also apparent in his Thanksgiving Day Proclamation issued on October 3, 1789, shortly after he became president. He obviously saw that the two-fold attitude of faith and thanksgiving toward God would be the tie that would bind the new nation together. After declaring it being the duty of all nations to "acknowledge the providence of Almighty God and obey His will," he gave a reason for this special day of Thanksgiving, saying,

> That we may then unite in most humbly offering our prayers and supplications to the Great Lord and Ruler of Nations and beseech him to pardon our national sins and other transgressions, to enable us all, whether in public or private stations, to perform our several and relative duties properly and punctually, to render our national government a blessing to all people, by constantly being a government of wise, just and constitutional laws, discreetly and faithfully executed and obeyed.[176]

Washington's sacrificial service and his bravery in battle endeared him to the hearts of the founding generation and he was twice elected unanimously to serve as the President of the new nation. The founding generation said this of him:

First in war; first in peace;
and first in the hearts of his countrymen.

---

[175] William J. Johnson, *George Washington, the Christian* (New York: Abingdon Press, 1919), 24-35.

[176] https://www.mountvernon.org/education/primary-sources-2/article/thanksgiving-proclamation-of-1789/

Benjamin Franklin

Benjamin Franklin (1709-1790) is often considered one of the least religious of the Founding Fathers. In his early years, he did entertain Deistic views about God and the Bible. However, his religious sentiments and views changed through the years, attributable, no doubt, to his Puritan roots, his exposure to the Great Awakening, and his friendship with George Whitefield.

Franklin was born into a Puritan home in Boston and the evidence suggests that his forebears were Separatist Puritans on both sides of the family. He refers to them as "dissenting Protestants" and he tells how his father, Josiah Franklin, fled England in 1685, with his first wife and three small children, in order to escape religious persecution. Franklin says in his *Autobiography* that they came under persecution in England because of their attendance at *conventicles,* which were religious gatherings that had been outlawed by the British government. [177]

Franklin, a voracious reader as a child, was exposed to Deism by reading religious treatises against it. He later read books by Deists, and by the age of seventeen, had decided that he was a Deist. However, by the time Whitefield and the Awakening arrived in Philadelphia in 1739, Franklin had

---

[177] Benjamin Franklin, *The Autobiography of Benjamin Franklin* (New York: Airmont, 1965), 13-15; quoted in Hyatt, *The Faith & Vision of Benjamin Franklin* (Grapevine, TX: Hyatt Press, 2015), 10-12.

already moved away from Deism, deciding that it did not provide motivation for the ethical and moral behavior necessary for a stable society.[178]

Franklin embraced both Whitfield and the Great Awakening. In fact, he and Whitefield became close friends and business partners, with Franklin taking on the task of printing and selling Whitefield's sermons and journals. He also advised Whitefield in business matters, including Whitefield's vision for an orphanage in Georgia.

In his *Autobiography,* Franklin refers to Whitefield as "a perfectly honest man," and he describes their friendship as being "sincere on both sides, which lasted till his death."[179] Whitefield stayed in Franklin's home while visiting Philadelphia, and it is obvious that, in spite of their differences, their friendship ran deep. Franklin wrote to his brother James, a printer in Boston, saying, "Whitefield is a good man and I love him."[180]

Whitfield's influence on Franklin was obvious. For example, in a 1756 letter, Franklin presented a proposal to Whitefield that they partner in establishing a new colony in Ohio. This colony would honor God and advance the Christian faith. He wrote,

> I imagine we could do it effectually and without putting the nation at too much expense. What a glorious thing it would be, to settle in that fine country a large strong body of religious and industrious people! What a security to the other colonies; and advantage to Britain, by increasing her

---

[178] Hyatt, *The Faith & Vision of Benjamin Franklin,* 26.

[179] Franklin, 102.

[180] Hyatt, *The Faith & Vision of Benjamin Franklin,* 38.

people, territory, strength and commerce. Might it not greatly facilitate the introduction of pure religion among the heathen, if we could, by such a colony, show them a better sample of Christians than they commonly see in our Indian traders, the most vicious and abandoned wretches of our nation?[181]

Comparing his life to a drama and himself in the "final act," Franklin explained that he would like to "finish handsomely" by giving himself to such a project. "In such an enterprise," he said, "I could finish my life with pleasure, and I firmly believe God would bless us with success."[182]

Commenting on Franklin's proposal, historian Thomas S. Kidd, wrote, "The printer may have doubted some specifics of Christian doctrine, but he hardly questioned the merit of working for God's honor and the public good."[183]

Kidd, however, has understated the significance of Franklin's proposal. It demonstrates that Franklin saw no conflict between faith and public affairs; in fact, his letter shows, yet again, that he considered Christianity necessary for a healthy and stable society. The fact that he wanted Whitefield to partner with him in this venture demonstrates his high regard for Whitefield and his commitment to the evangelical revivalism preached by Whitefield, to which he refers as "pure religion."

Franklin's commitment to Christian values for a stable society was also observable in his interaction with the well-known Deist, Thomas Paine. Although there are disagreements about

---

[181] Benjamin Franklin to Whitefield, July 2, 1756, Leonard W. Labaree, ed., *The Papers of Benjamin Franklin: April 1, 1755 through September 30, 1756* (New Haven: Yale Univ. Press, 2014), 138.

[182] Benjamin Franklin to Whitefield, 138-39.

[183] Kidd, *George Whitefield: America's Spiritual Founding Father*, 211.

the date of the following letter and whether Paine was the actual recipient, the evidence points to Paine as the recipient, probably in 1786 or 1787.

In the letter, Franklin is responding to a manuscript Paine sent in which he challenged the idea of a prayer-answering God, the deity of Christ, the inspiration of Scripture, and other aspects of orthodox Christianity. Franklin refused to print the book, and in very strong language, urged Paine not even to allow anyone else to see it. He wrote,

> I would advise you, therefore . . . to burn this piece before it is seen by any other person; whereby you will save yourself a great deal of mortification by the enemies it may raise against you, and perhaps a good deal of regret and repentance. If men are so wicked with religion [Christianity], what would they be if without it.[184]

Secularists love to point to a letter written by Franklin to President Ezra Stiles of Yale University, just a few weeks before Franklin's death. In it, Franklin expressed doubts about the divinity of Christ. It was in response to a letter Stiles had written to Franklin in which he specifically asked his opinion of Christ.

Franklin first addressed the morals of Jesus, saying, "I think the system of morals and his religion, as he left them to us, the best the world ever saw or is likely to see." Then, addressing the question of Jesus' divinity, Franklin chose not to give a clear, unambiguous opinion. He said, "I have, with most of the dissenters in England, some doubts as to his divinity,

---

[184] "Benjamin Franklin's Letter to Thomas Paine," https://wallbuilders.com/benjamin-franklins-letter-thomas-paine/

though it is a question I do not dogmatize on, having never studied it."[185]

Then, with his typical wit, he quipped, "I think it needless to busy myself with it now, when I expect soon an opportunity of knowing the truth with less trouble." He went on to say that he supported the doctrine of the divinity of Christ if it would make His teachings more respected and better observed.

The dialogue raises questions. Was Franklin simply humoring Stiles who may have been influenced by the negative influences of the Enlightenment? Was he catering to Stiles' doubts in order to avoid a bothersome debate? The fact is that Franklin had clearly stated his view of Christ in a debate over the dismissal of a Presbyterian pastor many years before this letter to Stiles.

The case involved Samuel Hemphill, Pastor of the First Presbyterian Church in Philadelphia where Franklin had attended before he met Whitefield. When Hemphill was dismissed in 1735 for allegedly emphasizing good works over Christ's atonement, Franklin came to his defense. Demonstrating an impressive depth of faith and understanding, he wrote,

> Let us then consider what the Scripture Doctrine of this Affair is, and in a Word it is this: Christ by his Death and Sufferings has purchased for us those easy terms and conditions of our acceptance with God, proposed in the Gospel, to wit, Faith and Repentance: By his Death and Sufferings, he has assured us of God's being ready and willing to

---

[185] Franklin to Stiles, https://www.constitution.org/primarysources/franklin-stiles.html.

accept of our sincere, though imperfect obedience to his revealed will; By his Death and Sufferings he has atoned for all sins forsaken and amended, but surely not for such as are willfully and obstinately persisted in . . . and that the ultimate End and Design of Christ's Death, of our Redemption by his Blood, was to lead us to the Practice of all Holiness, Piety and Virtue, and by these Means to deliver us from future Pain and Punishment, and lead us to the Happiness of Heaven, may, (besides what has been already suggested) be proved from innumerable Passages of the holy Scriptures.[186]

Although Franklin stopped attending First Presbyterian Church in Philadelphia over this issue, he heartily attended other meetings, such as those of Whitefield. And when he learned that his daughter had stopped attending church because of a personal dislike for the minister, Franklin wrote her a letter in which he exhorted her on "the necessity and duty of attending church."[187] In regards to her not liking the minister, with typical wit, he reminded her, "Pure water is often found to have come through very dirty earth.[188]

Franklin was an avid reader of the Bible and would often quote Scripture in his writings and conversations. He also kept certain Christian events and festivals as was made clear in the context of his telling of the positive health benefits he had experienced from a vegetarian diet he had once practiced. He then remarked that he celebrated Lent

---

[186] "A Defense of Mr. Hemphill's Observations, [30 October 1735]," *Founders Online*, National Archives, https://founders.archives.gov/documents/Franklin/01-02-02-0011.

[187] Franklin, 79.

[188] Franklin, 79.

by returning to his vegetarian diet. He wrote, "I have since kept several Lents most strictly, leaving the common diet for that."[189]

In 1757, he sailed to England. One night, during the trip across the Atlantic, the ship almost crashed into a small, rocky island. After arriving safely, Franklin wrote a letter to his wife, in which he said,

> The bell ringing for church, we went thither immediately, and with hearts full of gratitude, returned sincere thanks to God for the mercies we had received. If I were a Roman Catholic, perhaps I should, on this occasion, vow to build a chapel to some saint; but as I am not, if I were to vow at all, it should be to build a light house.[190]

On June 28, 1787, seventeen years after the death of Whitefield, the Constitutional Convention was about to be suspended because of unresolved dissension. It was a critical moment! Franklin, now 81 years of age, rose to his feet and addressed George Washington, the Convention's President, with these words:

> How has it happened, sir, that we have not hitherto once thought of humbly appealing to the Father of lights to illuminate our understandings? In the beginning of the contest with Great Britain, when we were sensible to danger, we had daily prayers in this room for Divine protection. Our prayers, sir, were heard and they were graciously answered. I have lived, sir, a long time and the longer I live, the more

---

189 Franklin, 42.
190 Franklin, 159.

convincing proofs I see of this truth—that God governs in the affairs of men. And if a sparrow cannot fall to the ground without his notice, is it probable that an empire can rise without His aid? We have been assured, sir, in the sacred writings that *except the Lord build the house, they labor in vain that build it*. I firmly believe this. I therefore beg leave to move that, henceforth, prayers imploring the assistance of heaven and its blessing on our deliberation be held in this assembly every morning before we proceed to business.[191]

The notion that Franklin was a Deist who would not want faith in God to be a part of public proceedings is based on either a lack of knowledge or a distortion of the facts. Franklin, like the other Founders, believed Christian morality to be absolutely necessary for a stable and prosperous society.

James Madison

James Madison (1751-1836) is best known as the chief architect of the Constitution and the fourth President of the United States. He was a devout Christian, trained in the College of New Jersey, formerly the Log College, a center of religious activity during the Great Awakening. The spiritual climate of the college just prior to Madison's enrolment is described in a letter (dated April 16, 1757), to the revivalist, Samuel Davies, from Samuel Finley, a trustee of the college:

---

[191] Hyatt, *The Faith & Vision of Benjamin Franklin*, 62-63.

Our glorious Redeemer has poured out His Holy Spirit upon the students at our College. The whole house was a Bochim (place of weeping). Mr. William Tennant, who was on the spot, says that there never was, he believes, more genuine sorrow for sin and longing after Jesus.[192]

As a Virginian, Madison was expected to attend the College of William and Mary in Williamsburg, but instead, he chose to attend the College of New Jersey, later renamed Princeton University. Perhaps this was due to both its strong Christian stance and the reputation of its president, John Witherspoon (1723–1794). Witherspoon, who had been trained at the University of Edinburgh in Scotland, came to the Colonies for the express purpose of serving as the College President. In this influential position, he both advised and taught many of the Founding Fathers. He was also a signer of the Declaration of Independence (1776). Madison was his most famous student.

Following graduation, Madison remained at the College of New Jersey for an additional year, during which time he translated the Bible from Hebrew and Greek into English. This work, together with the influence of his colleagues and teachers helped shape his worldview, one that was obviously influenced by the Great Awakening. This is why Dr. D. James Kennedy (1930-2007) and his co-worker, Dr. Jerry Newcombe, could confidently state, "Madison's political worldview was one shaped by the Bible more than any other source."[193]

---

[192] Charles G. Finney, *Revival Lectures* (Grand Rapids: Fleming H. Revell, n.d.), 531-32.

[193] D. James Kennedy with Jerry Newcombe, *What If America Were A Christian Nation Again?* (Nashville: Thomas Nelson, 2003), 89.

That Madison was a devout follower of Jesus is obvious from his many public and private writings. For example, in a letter to a friend, by the name of William Bradford, Madison encouraged him to be sure of his own salvation, saying,

> A watchful eye must be kept on ourselves lest, while we are building ideal monuments of renown and bliss here, we neglect to have our names enrolled in the Annals of Heaven."[194]

He also told Bradford of his desire that public officials would openly testify of their faith in Christ, and he encouraged Bradford to do so. He wrote,

> I have sometimes thought there could not be a stronger testimony in favor of religion than for men who occupy the most honorable and gainful departments . . . becoming fervent advocates in the cause of Christ; and I wish you may give your evidence in this way.[195]

In 1812, during his tenure as President, Madison signed a federal bill that provided economic aid to help a Bible society in mass distribution of the Bible. Also, throughout his presidency (1809-1816), he issued several proclamations for national days of prayer, fasting, and thanksgiving.

In later writings, Madison expressed doubts about the value of chaplains in the military and the proclamation of Days of Prayer and Thanksgiving. This was based, however, on his concern that the church not become dependent on civil

---

[194] http://www.faithofourfathers.net/madison.html.

[195] http://www.faithofourfathers.net/madison.html.

government. This was prompted, no doubt, by his knowledge of Christian history, knowledge he had gained from studying that history from the perspective of the Protestant Reformers. This alerted him to the specific, distinct roles the Reformers had assigned to the church and to civil government. This was known at the *Creator-Redeemer Distinction.*

In response to the church and state having been merged by Constantine and to the ensuing corruption of the church, the Reformers emphasized that God rules over two separate realms: the natural and the spiritual. One the one hand, all citizens—whether Christian or non-Christian—have a responsibility to relate to God as Creator in the natural or civil realm. On the other hand, Christians relate to God, not only as Creator, but also as Redeemer. So, the Reformers drew a clear line of distinction between the two. They asserted that the civil government should have no role in the church or in the spiritual life of the individual Christian. How a person related to God as Redeemer, they believed, was outside the jurisdiction of the civil government. This was the *Creator-Redeemer Distinction.*

Some of the Radical Reformers, such as the Quakers, Baptists, and Separatist Puritans, argued that the church should not accept any offer of support or sanction from the civil government. They argued that a church that becomes beholden to the government loses its ability to be a corrective voice to that government, because it has put itself in the precarious position of being dependent on that government for its security and well-being.

It was for this reason that the Puritans in New England would not allow their ministers to hold civil office. History had taught them that Christian leaders who are beholden to the state tend to become morally corrupt, and that pleasing those with civil power tends to become more important to them than pleasing God.

That this was Madison's concern is clearly borne out in his comments in his *Detached Memoranda* when he notes a failed attempt to include the words "Jesus Christ" in the preamble of a religious freedom bill in the Virginia state legislature. Madison was concerned that, by including the name of the "Savior" in a bill guaranteeing religious liberty, non-Christians would be discriminated against. He says,

> The opponents of the amendment turned the judgment of the House against it, by successfully contending that the better proof of reverence for that Holy Name would be not to profane it by making it a topic of legislative discussion and particularly by making His religion the means of abridging the rights of other men, in defiance of His own declaration that His kingdom was not of this world.[196]

Madison obviously raised these questions as one who wanted to protect both individual liberty and the purity of Christianity. That this was his concern is spelled out in a statement in 1822 to Edward Livingston. He wrote,

> We are teaching the world a great truth, that governments do better without kings and nobles than with them. The merit will be doubled by the other lesson: that Religion flourishes in greater purity without, than with the aid of government."[197]

---

[196] From Madison's "Detached Memoranda," http://candst.tripod.com/detach.htm

[197] Novak, 59-60.

Thomas Jefferson

Thomas Jefferson (1743-1826), along with Benjamin Franklin, is often regarded by secularists as one of the non-Christian Founders of the nation, a champion of the separation of church and state, and an advocate to keep religion out of government. Nothing could be further from the truth!

Jefferson was a life-long member of the Anglican Church, and while President, he sat on the front row during church services that were, in fact, held each Sunday in one of the chambers of the House of Representatives in Washington, D.C. At one point, displeased with the music, he ordered the Marine Band to be present in the services to provide music for the singing of psalms and hymns. This ensemble actually received its pay from the federal treasury. No one protested because none in that generation thought of removing God from the public life of the nation.

Jefferson was a member of the Virginia House of Burgesses, which was the elected legislative body of the Colony of Virginia. He also served as Governor (1779-1781). While serving in these offices, he fought for religious liberty, a position that required that the Anglican Church no longer be the official church of that Colony. Being the state church meant that it was legally supported by the required tithes of all residents. This requirement was opposed by many, especially non-Anglicans, who were called "dissenting Protestants" and who made up about three-quarters of Virginia's population.

Some have incorrectly interpreted Jefferson's efforts to disestablish the Anglican Church as a sign of his secularism. However, his effort was, in fact, an expression of both his faith and his support for the vision of the dissenting Protestant groups, which included Baptists, Quakers, Presbyterians and separatist Puritans. These dissenting Protestants strongly opposed the idea of the civil government having any role in matters of faith, as had been the case with churches in Europe, a practice that had begun with Constantine merging Christianity with the Empire.

In opposing the merger of faith with civil government, Jefferson clearly expresses his commitment to Christian truth. For example, in his 1777 *Bill for Religious Freedom*, he refers to Jesus as the "Holy Author of our religion." He writes,

> Whereas Almighty God hath created the mind free; that all attempts to influence it by temporal punishments or burdens, or by civil incapacitations, tend only to beget habits of hypocrisy and meanness, and are a departure from the plan of the Holy Author of our religion, who being Lord both of body and mind, yet chose not to propagate it by coercions on either, as was his Almighty power to do . . . that to compel a man to furnish contributions of money for the propagation of opinions which he disbelieves, is both sinful and tyrannical; that even forcing him to support this or that religious teacher is depriving him of the comfortable liberty of giving his contributions to the particular pastor whose morals he would make his pattern, and whose

powers he feels most persuasive to righteousness.[198]

Although in the latter part of his life, Jefferson expressed personal doubts about the Trinity and the deity of Christ, these doubts were expressed within the context of a life committed to a Christian worldview. Also, although he doubted the reality of miracles, he never considered himself an agnostic or Deist and he said, "I am a real Christian, that is to say, a disciple of the doctrines of Jesus."[199]

Jefferson's actions clearly demonstrate that he welcomed Christian influence in the public and political arenas and that he saw no problem with the government advancing Christian causes. For example, as President, Jefferson negotiated a federal treaty with the Kaskaskia Indian Tribe, a treaty that, among other things, stipulated that federal funds be made available to pay for a Christian missionary to work with this tribe and for the building of a Christian church in which they could worship.

It should also be noted that the so-called *Jefferson Bible* was not an effort—as the name suggests—on Jefferson's part to produce his own Bible. He himself did not call it a Bible. The title *Jefferson Bible* is, in fact, misleading. Jefferson's title was *The Life and Morals of Jesus of Nazareth,* and in it, he meticulously brings together the teachings of Jesus into a single volume that he intended primarily for evangelizing and instructing Native American tribes.

---

[198] "A Bill for Establishing Religious Freedom, 18 June, 1779, https://founders.archives.gov/documents/Jefferson/01-02-02-0132-0004-0082.

[199] Letter to Charles Thomson Monticello, June 19, 1816, http://www.let.rug.nl/usa/presidents/thomas-jefferson/letters-of-thomas-jefferson/jefl239.php.

He demonstrates his high regard for Jesus Christ by the manner in which he closed all presidential documents: "In the year of our Lord Christ." Also significant is his remark: "Of all the systems of morality that have come under my observations, none appear to me so pure as that of Jesus."[200]

In 1819, Jefferson founded the University of Virginia in Charlottesville, Virginia. At the same time, he invited all denominations and Christian sects to establish schools of instruction adjacent to or within the precincts of the university. He wrote,

> The students of the University will be free and expected to attend religious worship at the establishment of their respective sects, in the morning, and in time to meet their school at the University at its stated hour.[201]

The evidence is both plentiful and clear. Jefferson saw no problem with Christian influence in the public square, nor with the government advancing Christian causes. What he was against was the government dictating religious beliefs and religious practices, and favoring one church or denomination over another, and that is what the so-called *wall of separation* is all about.

The Truth about
The Wall of Separation

The term, *wall of separation*, has become commonplace in discussions about the relationship of church and state in

---

[200] Thomas Jefferson to William Camby, 18 Sept. 1813, *Writings*, XIII: 377; cited in D. James Kennedy, *What if America Were a Christian Nation Again* (Nashville: Thomas Nelson, 2003), 46.

[201] Hart, 351.

modern America. Jefferson is the one who first used the phrase. It is found in a letter he wrote to a group of Baptists on January 1, 1802. His purpose in writing the letter was to assure them that the First Amendment (1789) provided a "wall of separation" that would protect them from government intrusion. He was referring to the first part of the First Amendment that reads, "Congress shall make no law concerning the establishment of religion, or prohibiting the free exercise thereof."

Modern secularists have seized upon the phrase "wall of separation" and twisted it to mean something that Jefferson never intended. They assert, incorrectly, that it is a wall to keep expressions of faith out of government. This is a blatant distortion of Jefferson's words and intent.

Jefferson's historic exchange was with the Danbury Baptist Association of Connecticut whose members were concerned about their status in the new nation and how they would be treated. They had reason for concern, for throughout Europe, the Baptists had been an outlawed and severely persecuted Christian sect by both the state and the state-sanctioned churches, both Catholic and Protestant.

They had also suffered persecution in Colonial America, particularly in Virginia, at the hands of the Anglican Church which had been designated as the official, established church in Virginia. Subsequently, they wrote to Jefferson because they saw in him an ally and friend who, as Governor of Virginia, had come to their aid when they had been marginalized and persecuted by the state and its official church.

In his letter of response, Jefferson quoted the part of the Amendment that reads, "Congress shall make no law respecting an establishment of religion, or prohibiting the free exercise thereof." He assured the association that this meant that, in America, there would be "a wall of separation" that would protect them and any other religious group from the intrusion of the state.

Clearly, Jefferson understood the First Amendment to serve as a unidirectional wall, put in place to keep the government out of the church, not to keep God out of the government. His thinking in this regard reflects the Creator-Redeemer distinction of the Reformation that allowed the state no jurisdiction in matters of faith.

Jefferson's own actions consistently demonstrate that he did not see the First Amendment as blocking expressions of faith in public affairs, nor did it require the government to remain neutral in matters of faith. Indeed, his position was confirmed by Joseph Story (1779-1845) who served as a Supreme Court Justice for thirty-four years from 1811-1845. Commenting on the First Amendment, Story said,

> We are not to attribute this prohibition of a national religious establishment to an indifference in religion, and especially to Christianity, which none could hold in more reverence than the framers of the Constitution.[202]

Was Jefferson attempting to exclude Christian influence from the public and political arenas with his use of the term "wall of separation"? Absolutely not! Like Washington, Adams, Franklin and others, Jefferson did not want an official state church—as had been the case in Europe—monitoring the religious beliefs and activities of its citizenry.

---

[202] Joseph Story, *A Familiar Exposition of the Constitution of the United States* (New York: Harper & Brothers, 1847), 259-61.

John Witherspoon

John Knox Witherspoon (1723-1794) was the only ordained minister to sign the Declaration of Independence. As a delegate from New Jersey to the Continental Congress, he was one of its most outspoken and influential members, serving on over one hundred committees. He was involved in drafting the Articles of Confederation, and it was he who authored the calls to prayer and fasting that were published by the Congress during the Revolutionary War.

Witherspoon, a Scot, had been a well-known preacher and reformer in the Presbyterian Church in Scotland. A scholar with degrees from both the University of St. Andrews and the University of Edinburgh, he was highly respected for his vast knowledge. Committed to a Christian worldview, he once proclaimed, "Cursed is all learning that is contrary to Christ." [203] In Scotland, Witherspoon had been a dissenting Protestant, advocating for Biblical reform in both the church and civil government. His efforts provoked reaction from the authorities, and consequently, he spent time in prison for his faith. So, he knew by experience the importance of freedom of conscience and religious liberty. He knew that true Christianity was the only source of genuine freedom, and he expressed this in the following statement:

God, grant that in America true religion and civil

---

[203] D. James Kennedy and Jerry Newcombe, *What if the Bible Had Never Been Written* (Nashville: Thomas Nelson, 1998), 89.

liberty may be inseparable, and that unjust attempts to destroy the one, may in the issue tend to the support and establishment of both.[204]

Having experienced oppression in Scotland from the British Crown, Witherspoon was appalled by King George III's ever increasing intrusion into the affairs of the Colonies. He was especially troubled and alarmed by reports that Anglican bishops were to be sent to the Colonies. Consequently, in 1774, he joined the Committees of Correspondence, the venue developed as a means of sharing ideas and information with one another throughout the colonies.

In his 1776 sermon *The Dominion of Providence Over the Passions of Men*, Witherspoon presented a Biblical justification for a defensive war with Great Britain, as well as a reason to expect victory. It was published and widely distributed. Knowing his prominence at the Continental Congress, it is likely that this sermon was influential in the prominent use of the word "Providence" in the Declaration of Independence.

Witherspoon's influence in America's founding was immense. As President and lecturer at the College of New Jersey, he personally taught and mentored many of the country's earliest leaders. Of his students, 37 became judges (three of whom served on the Supreme Court); 12, members of the Continental Congress; 28, senators; and 49, congressmen. He personally mentored James Madison, the fourth President and chief architect of the U.S. Constitution. It is not surprising, then, that he has been called, "The most influential academic in American history." [205]

---

[204] William Novak, *On Two Wings: Humble Faith and Common Sense at the American Founding* (San Francisco: Encounter Books, 2002), 16.

[205] Novak, 15.

Would Witherspoon have supported or promoted a secular government that excluded Christianity from the public square? Absolutely not!

Benjamin Rush

Benjamin Rush (1745-1813) was a member of the Continental Congress and a signer of the Declaration of Independence. Dr. Rush had earned his M.D. at the University of Edinburgh. After immigrating to the Thirteen Colonies, he had served as Surgeon General for the Revolutionary Army. Not only was he one of Philadelphia's leading citizens, but he also served as Professor of Chemistry and Medical Theory at the University of Pennsylvania.

Rush was a devout Christian and was convinced that the American Republic could not survive apart from Christian values and morality. In 1806, he proposed inscribing John 3:17 above the doors of courthouses and other public buildings. The passage reads, *The Son of Man Came into the World, Not To Destroy Men's Lives, But To Save Them.*

Rush was convinced that the founding documents were a work of God. Careful not to put them on the same level as Scripture, he, nonetheless, said,

> I do not believe that the Constitution was the offspring of inspiration, but I am as perfectly satisfied that the Union of the United States in its form and adoption is as much the work of a Divine Providence as any of the miracles recorded in the Old and New Testament.[206]

---

[206] Benjamin Rush: Observations on the Fourth of July Procession in Philadelphia, *Pennsylvania Mercury*, 15 July 1788, https://archive.csac.history.wisc.edu/benjamin_rush7.15.88.pdf.

Rush was also an ardent abolitionist and helped found the first Abolition society in America. He referred to slavery as a "hydra sin" and he helped the black preacher, and former slave, Richard Allen, establish the first African Methodist Episcopal Church in Philadelphia in 1794. Allen was deeply grateful for Rush's assistance and later wrote,

> We had waited on Dr. Rush and Mr. Robert Ralston, and told them of our distressing situation. We considered it a blessing that the Lord had put it into our hearts to wait upon those gentlemen. They pitied our situation, and subscribed largely towards the church, and were very friendly towards us and advised us how to go on . . . Dr. Rush did much for us in public by his influence. I hope the name of Dr. Benjamin Rush and Mr. Robert Ralston will never be forgotten among us. They were the two first gentlemen who espoused the cause of the oppressed and aided us in building the house of the Lord for the poor Africans to worship in. Here was the beginning and rise of the first African church in America.[207]

Rush once said, "I have alternately been called an Aristocrat and a Democrat. I am neither. I am a Christocrat."[208] His deep, Christ-centered faith is obvious in a letter he wrote to his wife during his final illness. He first addressed her personally, saying, "My excellent wife, I must leave you, but God will take care of you." He then continued in what could be called a eulogy of praise to God, saying,

> In the mystery of Thy holy incarnation, by Thy holy

---

[207] https://en.wikipedia.org/wiki/Benjamin_Rush.
[208] Federer, 544.

nativity; by Thy baptism, fasting, and temptation; by Thy agony and bloody sweat; by Thy cross and passion; by Thy precious death and burial; by Thy glorious resurrection and ascension, and by the coming of the Holy Spirit, blessed Jesus, wash away all my impurities, and receive me into Thy everlasting kingdom.[209]

Would Benjamin Rush have gone along with banning prayer and Bible reading from public venues? Obviously not!

Charles Carroll

Charles Carroll (1737-1832) was the sole Founding Father who was a Roman Catholic. A wealthy landowner in Maryland, he was not interested in politics initially. But because of attempts by King George and the British to impose heavy taxes and to regulate the lives of the Colonists, he became a vocal critic. His bold advocacy for independence brought him to the attention of other patriots, and he soon found himself welcomed by others of like mind. As a result, he was a delegate to the Continental Congress, as well as a signer of the Declaration of Independence. Later, he served as a senator from Maryland.

Carroll expressed a deep faith in Jesus Christ, perhaps showing the influence of the Awakening, with its emphasis on faith in Christ, rather than on religious ritual and church affiliation.

---

[209] William J. Federer, *America's God and Country: Encyclopedia of Quotations* (St. Louis, MO: Amerisearch, 2013), 544.

In a letter to a friend, he declared, "On the mercy of my Redeemer I rely for salvation and on His merits; not on the works I have done in obedience to His precepts."[210]

By 1826, Carroll was the last surviving signer of the Declaration of Independence. Consequently, that year, New York City requested from him a copy of the document for public display. In complying with the request, he added the following comment to the document:

> Grateful to Almighty God for the blessings which, through Jesus Christ our Lord, He has conferred on my beloved country in her emancipation and on myself in permitting me, under circumstances of mercy, to live to the age of eighty-nine years, and to survive the fiftieth year of American independence. I do hereby recommend to the present and future generations the principles of that important document as the best inheritance their ancestors could bequeath to them, and pray that the civil and religious liberties they have secured to my country may be perpetuated to remotest posterity and extended to the whole family of man.[211]

Although America was obviously founded on the philosophical and theological presuppositions of the Radical Reformation,[212] Roman Catholics soon came to see the value

---

[210] Letter from Charles Carroll to Charles W. Wharton, found in Barton, *The Role of Pastors & Christians in Civil Government*, 27.

[211] B. F. Morris, *Christian Life and Character of the Civil Institutions of the United States* (Philadelphia: George W. Childs, 1861), 147.

[212] The Radical Reformers were the Separatist Puritans, Quakers, Baptists, and others who rejected the medieval idea of a state-sponsored church. For an overview of the Radical Reformers, see Hyatt, *Pilgrims and Patriots*, 54-68.

of what has since been referred to as the unique American political experiment.

Catholic scholar, William Novak, has highlighted this in his excellent book entitled *On Two Wings: Humble Faith and Common Sense at the American Founding*. For example, in it, he cites Pope John Paul II (1920-2005), who praised America's founding and noted the responsibility of each generation to understand and embrace the nation's founding principles. John Paul wrote,

> The continuing success of American democracy depends on the degree to which each new generation, native-born and immigrant, makes its own the moral truths on which the Founding Fathers staked the future of your Republic."[213]

Influenced by the Enlightenment?

In addition to the Bible, the Founders often quoted classical writers and philosophers of the Enlightenment (1715-1789). This was an intellectual and philosophical movement that dominated the world of ideas for a time in Europe. Its ideas, emphasizing individualism, reason, and skepticism, challenged traditional religious views.

One of the most widely regarded and most influential thinkers of the Enlightenment was the British philosopher, John Locke (1632-1704). Because the Founders seemed to be particularly fond of the him, secularists have seized on this as evidence of the Enlightenment's pervasive influence on the Founders.

Clearly, this interpretation is based on either a lack of

---

[213] Novak, 95.

knowledge and understanding or on a biased twisting of the facts. It is true that the Founders quoted both Enlightenment and pagan philosophers, but this merely reflects their excellent, liberal arts education in classical history and philosophy. The people of Colonial America were, in fact, probably the best educated in the world at the time of the American Revolution.

In addition, regarding Locke, it should be noted that he was thoroughly Christian in his thinking. Born of Puritan stock, his social and political theories, such as *the social-compact theory* and the idea that "those who govern must do so only with the consent of the governed" were more a product of the Separatist Puritan tradition than of the Enlightenment. He emphasized reason, but he believed that honest reasoning would lead to a belief in the existence of the God of the Bible.

In his book, *The Reasonableness of Christianity*, Locke utilizes both reason and the revelation of Scripture to make his case for the veracity of Christianity. Arguing from Scripture and miracles, he writes,

> The evidence of Our Savior's mission from heaven is so great, in the multitude of miracles He did, before all sorts of people, that what He delivered cannot but be received as the oracles of God. For the miracles He did were so ordered by the divine providence and wisdom, that they never were, nor could be denied by any of the enemies or opposers of Christianity.[214]

---

[214] John Locke, *The Reasonableness of Christianity* (Stanford: Stanford Univ. Press, 1958), 57.

Concerning reason, Locke insisted that the pagan world remained in darkness because they made so little use of their ability to reason. Instead of using their rational faculties, which would lead them to the one true God, they allowed themselves to be bound by animal passions such as lust, fear, anger, and carelessness, which then made them vulnerable to false religions. "It was in this state of darkness and error," said Locke, "that our Savior found the world."[215]

Clearly, then, Locke's influence, was not *away from* Christianity, but rather, *toward* Christianity, resulting in a political system that was based on both revelation and reason.

He Smiled on Our Beginnings

We are not claiming that all the Founders were committed evangelical Christians. We find among them a variety of church affiliations and various levels of piety and devotion. We do assert, however, that all were committed to a Christian worldview and all believed that only the teachings of Jesus provided the moral underpinnings for a successful nation.

In discussing the faith of Patrick Henry (1736-1799), an anonymous author, writing in a 1956 edition of *The Virginian*, noted how Henry had expressed his deep Christian faith in his will. Henry, who served as governor of Virginia and signed the Declaration of Independence, wrote,

> I have now disposed of all my property to my family. There is one thing more I wish I could give them, and that is the Christian Religion. If they had that and I had not given them one shilling they would have

---

[215] Locke, 57.

161

been rich; and if they had not that and I had given them all the world, they would be poor.

This writer rightly concludes that Henry's faith was, more or less, the norm for the founding generation, and writes,

> It cannot be emphasized too strongly or too often that this great nation was founded not by religionists but by Christians—not on religion but on the Gospel of Jesus Christ.[216]

The Founders expressed their collective belief that God was intimately involved in the birth of the nation when, in creating the official seal of the nation, they chose to inscribe the Latin words, *Annuit Coepits*, meaning, "He Smiled on Our Beginnings."[217]

Under the statement, the Founders included the eye to symbolize the all-seeing eye of Providence.

---

[216] *The Virginian*, April 1956, vol. II no, 3.
[217] Novak, 2.

Chapter 12

The Marriage of Faith and Civil Liberty

> The highest glory of the American Revolution is this:
> it connected, in one indissoluble bond,
> the principles of civil government
> with the principles of Christianity.
>
> *John Quincy Adams (1767-1848)*

Faith and freedom were married in the thinking of America's founding generation. Civil liberty, they believed, could not exist apart from Christian morality. They would all agree with Benjamin Rush who declared,

> The only foundation for a republic is to be laid in Religion [Christianity]. Without this there can be no liberty, and liberty is the object and life of all republican governments.[218]

Expressions, such as, *One Nation Under God,* which is found in the Pledge of Allegiance; *In God We Trust,* found

---

[218] Benjamin Rush, *Essays, Literary, Moral, and Philosophical,* Philadelphia, 1798: "Of the Mode of Education Proper in a Republic," vol. 4 of *The Annals of America,* 20 vols. (Chicago: Encyclopedia Britannica, 1968), 28-29.

on all U.S. currency; and *God Bless America,* a common expression of presidents and politicians, are remnants of the faith of the Founders in whose generation God and civil liberty were intertwined.

They Believed that Christianity Works

The Founders believed that Christianity was advantageous and, in fact, necessary for a stable and prosperous society. Because of this, critics have accused them of being utilitarian in their faith. In other words, they assert that the Founders embraced Christianity merely because it worked to serve their purposes. In pushing back against such criticism, Novak points out that it would be odd if there were no advantage in following God's principles. He says,

> The Hebrew and Christian religions are, in fact, useful guides to living a good personal life. They are also good maps for how to make a republic work, not in some utopian future, but in this present world of sinful and fallen human beings.[219]

This is what the Founders believed. John Adams voiced this very perspective two weeks before the signing of the Declaration of Independence (1776). In a letter to his cousin, Zabdiel Adams, a minister of the Gospel, Adams exhorted him concerning his vital role in the new nation. He wrote,

> Statesmen, my dear Sir, may plan and speculate for Liberty, but it is Religion and Morality alone, which can establish the Principles upon which Freedom can securely stand. The only foundation of a free

---

[219] Novak, 104.

Constitution, is pure Virtue . . . You cannot therefore be more pleasantly, or usefully employed than in the Way of your Profession, pulling down the Strong Holds of Satan.[220]

The Founders saw Christianity as offering the only moral and philosophical system that would undergird the nation they had formed. George Washington made this clear in his Farewell Address.

Washington's Farewell Warning

In his Farewell Address in 1796, after serving two terms as America's first President, George Washington warned the young nation to guard against separating freedom from faith and supposing that morality could be maintained apart from Christian truth. He said,

> Of all the dispositions and habits which lead to political prosperity, religion and morality are *indispensable* supports. In vain would that man claim the tribute of patriotism, who should labor to subvert these great pillars of human happiness, these firmest props of the duties of men and citizens. The mere politician, equally with the pious man, ought to respect and to cherish them. And let us with caution indulge the supposition that morality can be maintained without religion [Christianity]. Whatever may be conceded to the influence of refined education on minds of peculiar structure, reason and experience both forbid us to expect that national morality can prevail in exclusion of religious principle.

---

[220] John Adams to Zabdiel Adams, 21 June 1776, https://founders.archives.gov/documents/Adams/04-02-02-0011.

When the Founders use the word *religion,* they are referring to Christianity specifically, not to religion, in general. Note that Washington does NOT say that *religion (i.e,* Christianity) is something to be tolerated in the new nation. Rather, he says that it is *indispensable.* In other words, he warns against any attempt to separate God from the state; that is, he is warning against trying to secularize the American political system.

Notice also, that Washington rejects the idea that national morality can be experienced apart from faith. Like the other Founders, Washington believed that only Christianity offered the spiritual, moral, and philosophical underpinnings for a prosperous and stable society.

A French Visitor Sees the Link Between Faith and Freedom

That faith and freedom were married in America was obvious to the French sociologist, Alexis de Tocqueville (1805-1859) who, in 1831, visited America to study her institutions. He wanted to see if he could discover the reason for America's rapidly achieved affluence and rise to power in the world.

Arriving in 1831, as the Second Great Awakening (1795-1835) was ebbing, he exclaimed, "The religious atmosphere of the country was the first thing that struck me on arrival in the United States." His observations led him to conclude that Americans had so completely merged Christianity and civil liberty in their thinking that it was impossible to make them conceive of one without the other.

According to Tocqueville, this linking of faith with civil liberty was the reason for their passion to spread the Gospel to the American frontier where new settlements were springing up. He wrote,

> I have known of societies formed by the Americans to send out ministers of the Gospel in the new Western states, to found schools and churches there, lest religion should be suffered to die away in those remote settlements, and the rising states be less fitted to enjoy free institutions than the people from whom they came. I met with New Englanders who abandoned the country in which they were born in order to lay the foundations of Christianity and of freedom on the banks of the Missouri, or in the prairies of Illinois. Thus, religious zeal is warmed in the United States by the fires of patriotism.[221]

Tocqueville, observing the close tie between faith and civil liberty, mused that that the means used to improve the political system were the same means employed in conversion and the advancement of the Christian faith. From his observations, he concluded, "From the beginning, politics and religion contracted an alliance which has never been dissolved."

Christianity and Civil Liberty Are Intertwined

The Christian commitment and mindset of the Founders was verified in a ten-year project to discover where they got their

---

[221] W. Cleon Skousen, *The 5000 Year Leap* (USA: National Center for Constitutional Studies, 1991), 84.

ideas for America's founding documents. The study found that, by far, the single most cited authority in their writings was the Bible.[222]

John Adams (1735-1826), one of the Founding Fathers, went on to serve as the second President of the United States (1797-1801). Nearly four decades after the American Revolution, Adams said,

> The general principles on which the Fathers achieved independence were the general principles of Christianity. Now I will avow that I then believed, and now believe, that those general principles of Christianity are as eternal and immutable as the existence and attributes of God.[223]

Further, in a 1798 speech to the officers of the Massachusetts Militia, Adams clearly reiterated the common belief of the founding generation that civil liberty and Christian morality are inseparable. They believed that the loss of the latter, would inevitably lead to the loss of the former. This is the basis on which Adams declared,

> We have no government armed with power capable of contending with human passions unbridled by morality and religion . . .. Our Constitution was made only for a moral and religious people. It is wholly inadequate to the government of any other."[224]

---

[222] Donald S. Lutz, "The Relative Influence of European Writers on Late Eighteenth Century American Political Thought," *America Political Science Review*, vol. 78, March 1884, 191.

[223] From John Adams to Massachusetts Militia, 17 October 1798, https://founders.archives.gov/documents/Adams/99-02-02-3102.

The Testimony of a Chief Justice

That America was founded on Christian ideals that emerged from the Great Awakening is obvious, not only from the testimonies of the Founders themselves, but also from the testimonies of those who were closest to them. A good example of such a person is John Marshall (1755-1835), who served as the second Chief Justice of the Supreme Court for thirty-four  years (1801-1835). Many consider him the greatest Chief Justice the Court has known. During his tenure, he heard many cases and offered groundbreaking opinions that continue to guide the Supreme Court and the United States Government today.

In one of his writings, Marshall clearly states what every Founder assumed: The founding documents and institutions on which the nation was formed assume a commitment to Christian principles and values. He wrote,

> No person, I believe, questions the importance of religion in the happiness of man, even during his existence in this world. The American population is entirely Christian, and with us Christianity and religion are identified. It would be strange, indeed, if with such a people, our institutions did not presuppose Christianity, and did not refer to it, and exhibit relations with it.[225]

---

[225] Robert Faulkner, *The Jurisprudence of John Marshall* (Westport, CT: Greenwood Press, 1968), 139.

While serving as Chief Justice, Marshall made the Supreme Court facilities available to a local congregation for their Sunday gatherings. So, each Sunday, the singing of Christian hymns and the preaching of God's Word could be heard ringing through the chambers of both the House of Representatives and the Supreme Court. This was neither surprising nor offensive because it corresponded with the mindset of the founding generation, a generation within which faith and freedom were as one.

The U.S. Supreme Court Makes a Clear Statement

From the discovery of this continent to the present hour, there is a single voice making this affirmation, this is a religious [Christian] people. There is a universal language pervading them all, having one meaning. They affirm and reaffirm that this is a religious nation . . .. The churches and church organizations which abound in every city, town, and hamlet; the multitude of charitable organizations existing everywhere under Christian auspices; the gigantic missionary associations, with general support, and aiming to establish Christian missions in every quarter of the globe. These, and many other matters which might be noticed, add a volume of unofficial declarations to the mass of organic utterances that this is a Christian nation.[226]

Although a form of this quotation was included in the first

---

[226] Church of the Holy Trinity v. United States, 143 U.S. 457 (1892), https://supreme.justia.com/cases/federal/us/143/457/.

chapter, it is appropriate to include it again here to demonstrate the Christian mindset of American culture as recently as 1892. In the ruling, *Church of the Holy Trinity vs The United States*, the nation's highest court ruled against the U.S. government, which had blocked an Anglican church from bringing in a foreign rector for their congregation. The government made this decision based on an immigration statute that limited the import of cheap labor.

The Court, however, ruled unanimously hat the statute did not apply to a church bringing in a minister of the Gospel because America is a Christian nation. In its ruling, the Court alluded to many of the historical records found in this volume. They also pointed out traditions, such as government functions, including court sessions, being opened with prayer and the invoking of the name of God in administering oaths.

In this ruling, the Supreme Court upheld the position that was understood for the first 150 years of the nation's existence: American liberty and Christian virtue are indissolubly linked.

This is why John Dickinson, Founding Father and chairman of the committee that produced the Articles of Confederation, warned that "when states lose their liberty, this calamity is generally owing to a decay of virtue."[227] And commenting on this fact, Novak is correct in declaring,

> Far from having a hostility toward religion, the Founders counted on religion [Christianity] for the underlying philosophy of the republic, its supporting ethic, and its reliable source of rejuvenation.[228]

---

[227], https://history.hanover.edu/courses/excerpts/334dickinson.html.
[228] Novak, 111.

The Key to Happiness

Clearly, the Founders believed that Christian principles and values were indispensable for happiness in this world. This is why they were not reticent about bringing their faith into the public arena. It is the reason that George Washington, in a meeting with Chiefs of the Delaware Indian Tribe, encouraged them to learn "above all the religion of Jesus Christ."

The Chiefs had come to meet with Congress, and they brought with them three of their youth, asking that they be educated in American schools. Washington addressed them as "Brothers" and referred to their mutual desire to "preserve the friendship between the Two Nations to the end of time." He expressed his hope that the Delaware would "become One people with your Brethren of the United States." He assured them that Congress would look upon their youth "as their own children." He then said,

> You do well to wish to learn our arts and our ways of life **and above all, the religion of Jesus Christ.** These will make you a greater and happier people than you are. Congress will do everything they can to assist you in this wise intention.[229]

This idea that Christian principles of morality are the key to happiness for both the individual and for society in general was a common belief of the founding generation. Tocqueville observed this phenomenon, and it amazed him. In Europe, religion and civil liberties were in opposition, but in America, he observed that the opposite was the case. .He wrote,

---

[229] Address to the Delaware Nation, 12 May 1779, https://founders.archives.gov/documents/Washington/03-20-02-0388.

Religion is necessary for the maintenance of republic institutions. That is not the view of one class or party among the citizens, but of the whole nation; it is found in all ranks.[230]

Recently, various Presidents have sought unsuccessfully to export American-style democracy to other nations, doing so apart from any connection to Christian faith and morality. The Founders would say that such efforts are futile, since true liberty cannot be had apart from Christian truth and morality.

This explains why John Hancock (1737-1793), President of the Second Continental Congress (1775-1781) and signer of the Declaration of Independence, wanted the entire earth to hear and embrace the Gospel of Jesus Christ. He expressed this in a Prayer Proclamation he issued while Governor of Massachusetts (1780-1785; 1787-1793). In the 1793 Proclamation, he declared,

> I do hereby appoint Thursday the eleventh day of April next, to be observed throughout this Commonwealth, as a day of solemn fasting, humiliation, and prayer . . . that with true contrition of heart we may confess our sins, resolve to forsake them, and implore the Divine forgiveness through the merits and mediation of JESUS CHRIST our Savior . . . and finally, to overrule all the commotion in the world, to the spreading of the true religion of our LORD JESUS CHRIST, in its purity and power, among all the people of the earth.[231]

---

[230] .Novak, 41.

[231] https://wallbuilders.com/proclamation-fasting-humiliation-prayer-1793-massachusetts.

Chapter 13

Remembering 1726

> When a nation goes down, or a society perishes,
> one condition may always be found;
> they forgot where they came from.
> They lost sight of what had brought them along.
>
> *Carl Sandburg (1878-1967)*

As the fires of Spiritual Awakening waned during and after the Revolutionary War, so did the anti-slavery sentiments it had fueled. The nation, however, could not forget 1726 and those anti-slavery embers would be fanned to flame—and more intensely so—as a Second Great Awakening erupted at the beginning of the 19th Century.

America's Second Great Awakening

The Second Great Awakening began on the East Coast in colleges such as, Yale, Dartmouth, and Columbia. At Yale, one-third of the 225 students were converted, and others were renewed in their faith during a revival in 1802. Revival erupted on other college campuses, as well, and many of these students became agents of revival throughout New England, Upstate New York, and on the Western Frontier. Noll says,

These college graduates did not so much create the local revivals, which had been taking place for decades in out-of-the-way rural villages, as they expanded their influence. Together with the promoters of local revivals, they spread concern for renewal up and down the East Coast. Soon there was hardly a locale in which Christians were not praying for revival or thanking God for having received one.[232]

The revival crossed the Allegheny Mountains and tamed the bawdy Western Frontier. At the great Cane Ridge Campmeeting in Bourbon County, Kentucky, in August of 1801, it was estimated that 25,000 people gathered for the event. It lasted several days and was characterized by great religious fervor, accompanied by weeping, trembling, laughing, and falling to the ground. Throughout the frontier, great interdenominational campmeetings, attended by Methodists, Baptists, Presbyterians, and others, became common.

Peter Cartwright (1785-1872), a circuit-riding, Methodist preacher of the era, said, "The work went on and spread almost in every direction gathering additional force till our country seemed all coming to God."[7]

The Second Great Awakening saved the nation from the negative influences of the French Revolution and Deism that had seeped into

---

[232] Noll, 169.

American culture during and after the Revolutionary War. It also revived the anti-slavery sentiments that had been such a great part of the First Great Awakening. Noll calls it "the most influential revival of Christianity in the history of the United States."[233]

Out of this Second Great Awakening, the 19th Century Abolition Movement emerged, the underground railroad was formed, and abolitionists, such as Harriet Tubman, Sojourner Truth, Frederick Douglass, Thomas Weld, and Charles Finney came on the scene.

Some may be surprised that Charles Finney (1792-1875) is on this list of 19th Century abolitionists, but Finney, best known for his revivalism, was, in fact, an outspoken opponent of slavery. He challenged the faith of professing Christians who defended slavery, saying, "It is impossible to be on the right side of God and the wrong side of the slavery issue." His convert, Thomas Weld, became a passionate abolitionist, and both worked hard to both convert sinners and end slavery.

When Finney was invited to be the first Professor of Systematic Theology at the newly formed Oberlin College, he did so only on the condition that "colored" people would be received "on the same conditions that we did white people, that there should be no discrimination made on account of color."[234] Oberlin became a center of revival and abolition, as well as an important link on the underground railroad, helping escaped slaves reach their destination in

---

[233] Noll, 166.

[234] Charles G. Finney, *The Original Memoirs of Charles G. Finney*, Garth M. Rosel and Richard A.G. Dupuis, eds. (Grand Rapids: Zondervan, 2002), 282.

the North or in Canada.

Each Generation Must Be Revived

Revivals have a life span, and by 1840 the Second Great Awakening was obviously fading. One writer has said,

> The need for another awakening was great. By 1845, the "aftershocks" of the Second Great Awakening had subsided. A low, lax state of religious feeling prevailed. Outward religion was still practiced, but the earlier power and vitality was gone.[235]

The fact remains, however, that 1726 had left an indelible imprint on America's national psyche and another Great Awakening would arise, renewing the American populace. So, in this final chapter, we will look at *The Great Prayer Awakening of 1857-58* and show how it helped end slavery and preserve the nation through its darkest hour—a horrible Civil War.

America's Third Great Awakening

In studying *The Great Prayer Awakening of 1857-58*, this writer has become convinced that it was, in fact, America's Third Great Awakening. To qualify as a Great Awakening, a revival should meet the following criteria, and this great Prayer Awakening certainly met each one.

1. It is an obvious sovereign work of God in that it has arisen apart from any identifiable human plan,

---

[235]

http://www.voiceoftheevangelists.com/Articles/HistoryofEvangelism/
THEGREATPRAYERREVIVALOF185758/tabid/466/Default.aspx

strategy, or design.

2. It is non-sectarian, touching people of all denominations and sects. No one group or church can "own" the revival.

3. It is not localized or regional, but instead, it has an obvious national impact on the nation and its culture.

The Great Prayer Awakening of 1857-58, began when a Dutch Reformed layman, Joseph Lanphier, began a daily noon prayer meeting in downtown New York City.[236] He invited local business people to spend their lunch hour praying for the conversion of the immigrants who were pouring into the city by the thousands, as well as for any personal requests that would be presented.

The format of the prayer meeting was simple. At 12 noon, the leader of the meeting would open with one or two verses of a well-known hymn, followed by an opening prayer, and then prayer requests would be presented. Anyone was then free to pray, share a prayer request, or give a testimony. No one was to take more than five minutes, and if anyone exceeded their allotted time, the leader would ring a bell, signaling for that person to conclude their prayer or comments.

The emphasis of the meeting was on the conversion of the

---

[236] Read a detailed account of this revival in my book, *The Great Prayer Awakening of 1857-58*, available from Amazon and at www.eddiehhyatt.com.

lost, and most of the prayers were directed to that end. Promptly at 1 p.m., the meeting was dismissed with a concluding prayer by the leader or someone appointed by the leader.

God's Power Is Manifest

Although bound by strict time restraints and held to a simple format, the meetings were accompanied by great spiritual power. God's presence permeated the atmosphere and significant answers to prayer occurred. People, as if drawn by an invisible force, came from all parts of the city to be in the prayer meeting.

Both Christians and nonbelievers attended the meetings, and many found Christ during the times of prayer. For example, a notorious criminal nicknamed *Awful Gardiner* came to the meeting and was gloriously saved and transformed. This created a great stir and news of the prayer meeting spread throughout the city and beyond.

From this prayer meeting on Fulton Street in Manhattan, a spirit of prayer seemed to be unleashed across the nation. Similar prayer meetings sprang up in such places as Boston, Philadelphia, Pittsburg, Cincinnati, Indianapolis, Chicago, Washington, D.C., as well as in many smaller cities and in rural areas.

Across the nation, people crowded into churches, fire stations, lodges, and halls to pour out their hearts to God in prayer. As God's Spirit was poured out, thousands came to Christ. The famous revivalist, Charles Finney (1792-1875), was still alive, and although he played no leading role in the revival, he noted that people preferred prayer meetings to conventional church services and that the general impression seemed to be, "We have had instruction until we are hardened; it is time for us to pray."[237]

Finney also told of a prayer meeting in Boston in which a man stood and declared that he had travelled almost 2000 miles from Omaha, Nebraska, and had found "a continuous prayer meeting all the way."[238]

All Segments of Society Impacted

The Prayer Revival had a profound impact on all sectors of the society. It was common for businesses to hang signs on their doors informing customers that they were closed for the noon prayer meeting. Meantime, newspapers carried regular reports of the revival and its progress. The editors of the daily *New York Herald* carried a regular section called "Revival Extras" by means of which they kept readers abreast of the latest revival news.

A Chicago newspaper carried a report showing the impact the revival was having on the society at large. It read,

> So far as the effects of the present religious movement are concerned, they are apparent to all. They are to be seen in every walk of life, to be felt in every place of society. The merchant, the farmer, the mechanic— all who have been within their influence—have been incited to better things; to a more orderly and honest way of life.[239]

---

[237] Charles G. Finney, *An Autobiography* (Old Tappan, NJ: Oberlin College, 1908), 444.

[238] Finney, 443.

[239] *America's Great Revivals* (Minneapolis: Bethany Fellowship, n.d.), 64-65.

In Chicago, a youthful D. L. Moody (1837-1899), who later became a renowned evangelist, attended daily prayer meetings. In a letter to his mother, he wrote, "Oh, how I do enjoy it! It seems as if God were here Himself." [240] In Washington, D.C., Presidents Franklin Pierce (1853-1857) and James Buchanan (1857-1861) attended prayer meetings that were organized there.

The Nation Is Awakened

One writer described what he called a "zone of heavenly influence" that pervaded the Eastern Seaboard and that extended out into the Atlantic Ocean, even affecting the passengers and crews of approaching ships. He wrote,

> Revival began aboard one ship before it reached the coast. People on board began to feel the presence of God and the sense of their own sinfulness. The Holy Spirit convicted them and they began to pray. As the ship neared the harbor, the captain signaled, "Send a minister." Another small commercial ship arrived in port with the captain, and every member of the crew converted in the last 150 miles. Ship after ship arrived with the same story: both passengers and crew were suddenly convicted of sin and turned to Christ before they reached the American coast. [241]

In Charleston, South Carolina, the pastor of the Anson Street Presbyterian Church, John L. Girardeau (1825-1898) established a prayer meeting in 1858 and exhorted his

---

[240] Malcolm McDow & Alvin L. Reid, *FireFall* (Nashville: Broadman & Holman, 1997), 266.

[241] www.truthkeepers.com/prayer.html.

people to "wait for the outpouring of the Holy Spirit."[242] The prayer service grew until the auditorium was overflowing with more than 2000 people. Although the Anson Street Church had been established for slaves, now whites, free blacks, and slaves all prayed together. As on the Day of Pentecost, the Holy Spirit suddenly fell upon them.

> They began to sob, softly, like the falling of rain; then, with deeper emotion, to weep bitterly, or to rejoice loudly, according to their circumstances. It was midnight before he could dismiss the congregation. The meeting went on night and day for weeks. Large numbers of both black and white were converted and joined churches in the city.[243]

Charles Finney described 1857-58 as a time when "a divine influence seemed to pervade the whole land."[244] He estimated that at the height of the revival 50,000 were being converted in a single week—and that was without the aid of modern communication and technology.

Conservative estimates place the total number of conversions at around one million, but some have suggested that as many as two million may have been converted. The March 1858, issue of a religious journal reported,

> The large cities and towns from Maine to California are sharing in this great and glorious work. There is hardly a village or town to be found where "a special divine power" does not appear displayed.[245]

---

[242] McDow & Reid, *FireFall*, 263.

[243] McDow & Reid, 263.

[244] Finney, *An Autobiography*, 444.

[245] http://www.praywithchrist.org/prayer/layman.php.

Mercy Precedes Judgement

Some have suggested that the Prayer Revival of 1857-58 was an outpouring of God's mercy preceding national judgment for the institutional sin of slavery—that it was, in fact, God giving the nation an opportunity to deal with this sin, and thereby, avoid the coming judgment. Others have insisted that it was God, in His mercy, releasing the spiritual and moral resources that would be necessary to survive the coming Civil War. Perhaps both theories are true. Regardless, up to this time, the slavery issue had not been dealt with and, on April 12, 1861, the first shot of the Civil War was fired, igniting the costliest war in American history.

Great loss of property and livelihood ensued, but it was minor compared to the tremendous loss of human life. The death toll is estimated to have ranged from 625,000 to over 700,000 soldiers and an unknown number of civilians. To these numbers must be added thousands of other casualties—those who were injured, disabled, and left helpless by the war. The magnitude of the loss is amplified by the fact that the population at the time was only 31 million.

By way of comparison, in the Viet Nam Conflict (1955-1975), 58,000 American soldiers lost their lives. In the more recent conflicts in Iraq and Afghanistan, fewer than 10,000 Americans have died. More lives were lost in the Civil War than were lost in all of the nation's wars combined, from the American Revolution through the Korean Conflict (1950-1953).

It was truly a time of deep grief and great devastation. Weeping could be heard in homes throughout the nation. In many families, both fathers and sons were missing. Hardly a family could be found that had not lost multiple family members. Was this the judgement of which George Mason

(1725-1792) and others had warned at the time of the nation's founding?

Only a few years after the Great Prayer Revival of 1857-1858, the nation was devastated by the Civil War of 1861-1865. Evidence suggests, however, that the spirit of prayer continued during the war in the North and the South and this, no doubt, preserved the people and the nation from utter ruin.

America Remembers Her Heritage

After two years of war, the Union had lost significant battles. The situation was grim, but fortunately, at this point, the nation remembered its godly heritage. Union leaders remembered 1726, and the U.S. Senate passed a resolution asking President Abraham Lincoln (1809-1865) to proclaim a national day of fasting and prayer. President Lincoln responded by designating April 30, 1863 as a national day of humiliation, prayer and the confession of national sins. This confession of sin included the sin of slavery. The President's powerful proclamation reads:

> *Whereas, the Senate of the United States devoutly recognizing the Supreme Authority and just Government of Almighty God in all the affairs of men and of nations, has, by a resolution, requested the President to designate and set apart a day for national prayer and humiliation:*

> *And whereas, it is the duty of nations as well as of men to own their dependence upon the overruling power of God, to confess their sins and transgressions in humble sorrow yet with assured hope that genuine repentance will lead to mercy and pardon, and to recognize the sublime truth, announced in the Holy Scriptures and proven by all history: that those nations only are blessed whose God is Lord:*

And, insomuch as we know that, by His divine law, nations like individuals are subjected to punishments and chastisement in this world, may we not justly fear that the awful calamity of civil war, which now desolates the land, may be but a punishment inflicted upon us for our presumptuous sins to the needful end of our national reformation as a whole people?

We have been the recipients of the choicest bounties of Heaven. We have been preserved these many years in peace and prosperity. We have grown in numbers, wealth and power as no other nation has ever grown.

But we have forgotten God. We have forgotten the gracious Hand which preserved us in peace and multiplied and enriched and strengthened us; and we have vainly imagined, in the deceitfulness of our hearts, that all these blessings were produced by some superior wisdom and virtue of our own.

Intoxicated with unbroken success, we have become too self-sufficient to feel the necessity of redeeming and preserving grace, too proud to pray to the God that made us!

It behooves us then to humble ourselves before the offended Power, to confess our national sins and to pray for clemency and forgiveness.

Now, therefore, in compliance with the request and fully concurring in the view of the Senate, I do, by this proclamation, designate and set apart Thursday, the 30th day of April, 1863, as a day of national humiliation, fasting and prayer.

And I do hereby request all the people to abstain on that day from their ordinary secular pursuits, and to unite, at their several places of public worship and their respective homes, in keeping the day holy to the Lord and devoted to the humble discharge of the religious duties proper to that solemn occasion.

All this being done, in sincerity and truth, let us then rest humbly in the hope authorized by the Divine teachings, that the united cry of the nation will be heard on high and answered with blessing no less than the pardon of our national sins and the restoration of our now divided and suffering country to its former happy condition of unity and peace.

In witness whereof, I have hereunto set my hand and caused the seal of the United States to be affixed. By the President: Abraham Lincoln.[246]

Because of 1726—the year that defined America—together with the nation's godly heritage and the recent Great Prayer Awakening (1857-1858), the people responded *en masse* to Lincoln's call to prayer. And after this day of repentance and prayer, there was an almost immediate turn of the war in favor of the North. But there would be one, final, severe test of faith.

In June 1863, Confederate General Robert E. Lee led 76,000 troops north into the Union territory of Pennsylvania. While the people were in a state of panic, Lincoln found solace in prayer. He later related his experience to General Daniel Sickles (1819-1914), who was wounded in the battle that ensued at Gettysburg. He said,

In the pinch of your campaign up there, when

---

[246] Digital copies of this Proclamation are readily available on the Internet.
http://www.abrahamlincolnonline.org/lincoln/speeches/fast.htm.

everybody seemed panic-stricken, and nobody could tell what was going to happen, oppressed by the gravity of our affairs, I went to my room one day, and locked the door, and got down on my knees before Almighty God, and prayed to Him mightily for victory at Gettysburg. I told Him that this was His war, and our cause His cause, but we couldn't stand another Fredericksburg or Chancellorsville. I then and there made a solemn vow to Almighty God, that if He would stand by our boys at Gettysburg, I would stand by Him. And afterward (I don't know how it was, and I can't explain it), soon a sweet comfort crept into my soul that God Almighty had taken the whole business into His own hands.[247]

At Gettysburg, The Union and Confederate armies battled for three days (July 1-3, 1863). By July 3, the Union forces had prevailed in a battle that proved to be the turning point of the war. Here, on November 19, 1863, President Lincoln delivered a brief speech, concluding ceremonies dedicating the battlefield cemetery. That speech has come to be known as the *Gettysburg Address.* It is one of the most significant speeches ever delivered by a national leader.

Some would suggest that the Union's victory at Gettysburg was coincidental, but the fact that it occurred on the heels of the national day of repentance, prayer and fasting, would suggest Divine intervention. Lincoln's amazing experience in prayer just before the battle also indicates that God intervened. One writer surmised that, in fact, the North did

---

[247] Robert R. Mathison, ed., *The Routledge Sourcebook of Religion and the American Civil Wa*r (New York: Routledge, Taylor & Francis Group, 2015), 280.

not win the Civil War, but rather, that prayer won the war. It happened because America remembered her revival heritage. She remembered 1726.

The War Ends and The Healing Continues

For all practical purposes, the war ended in the spring of 1865, when General Robert E. Lee and the last major Confederate army surrendered to General Ulysses S. Grant on April 9 at the Appomattox Courthouse in Virginia. Over the next few months, smaller units throughout the South laid down their arms and the bloodiest four years in American history finally came to an end.

Out of this environment of grave hostility and earnest prayer arose the Negro spiritual *Down By the Riverside*. The song included the phrase, *Ain't gonna study war no more,* and it captured the deepest feelings of many who longed for peace and a sense of God's blessing on the nation.

> *Gonna lay down my burdens,*
> *Down by the riverside,*
> *Down by the riverside, down by the riverside.*
> *Gonna lay down my burdens,*
> *Down by the riverside.*
> *Ain't gonna study war no more.*
>
> *Gonna sit down with Jesus,*
> *Down by the riverside,*
> *Down by the riverside, down by the riverside,*
> *Gonna sit down with Jesus,*
> *Down by the riverside.*
> *Ain't gonna study war no more.*

God Will Do It Again

At the present time, America is as divided, perhaps, as she has not been since the Civil War. And although demographics and culture have changed, the solution remains the same. We must remember our heritage. We must remember 1726.

In the same way that God spoke to ancient Israel in a critical time of national danger and spiritual apostasy, God is calling America to remember her heritage. The call is recorded in Isaiah 51:1-2:

> *Listen to Me, you who pursue righteousness and seek the LORD: Look to the rock from which you were cut and the quarry from which you were hewn; look to Abraham your father and Sarah, who gave you birth. When I called him he was only one man, and I blessed him and made him many.*

If the America of Washington, Jefferson, Lincoln, King, and of our grandparents and parents is to survive, we must remember our heritage. The needed change is not going to come as a result of a new church program, more entertaining church music, a new pastor, or a larger building. It will come as a result of a Visitation from Heaven in response to the desperate prayers of God's people. We must remember 1726, the year that defined America.

America's Future Is in Our Hands

The Awakening that will save America will not arise from a political process or party. It will begin, not at the White House, but at God's House. The promise of a national healing in II Chronicles 7:14 begins with the condition, *If My people. . . .* God did not say, "if the king," or "if the judges." He said, "If My people . . .." This means that America's future is in our hands.

This was powerfully illustrated by an event described by Dr. Billye Brim in her book, *First of All & the Awakenings*. She tells how, in 1979, she and about forty others had gathered to pray for the upcoming elections in the United States and for Israel.

As they "prayed up a storm" for the approaching election, the Spirit of God suddenly fell on her in a way that astonished her. She said that the words came with such power, "It was almost like I had to speak them or die." She found herself declaring,

> One thing will save America.
> And it is not the election.
> It is an Awakening to God.
> One thing will avail for Israel and the nations.
> It is an Awakening to God.[248]

She said, "These words shook us. Silenced us. Even rebuked us." They suddenly awakened to the reality of II Chronicles 7:14. They understood that, unless the people of God wake up and fulfill God's conditions for a national awakening and healing, the next election will be of little consequence.

Let us, therefore, reflect on how God has intervened again and again for this nation with mighty Visitations of His Presence and power. Let us remember 1726, and pray, "O Lord, do it once again!"

---

[248] Dr. Billye Brim, *First Things First & the Awakenings* (Joplin, MO: Billye Brim Ministries, 2017), 8.

Selected Bibliography

Amos, Gary and Richard Gardiner. *Never Before in History: America's Inspired Birth*. Richardson, TX: Food. for Thought and Ethics, 1998.

Barton, David. *The Role of Pastors & Christians in Civil Government*. Aledo, TX: Wallbuilders Press, 2003.

Edwards, Jonathan. *Jonathan Edwards on Revival*. Carlisle, PA: Banner of Truth Trust, 1994.

Federer, William J. *America's God and Country, Encyclopedia of Quotations*. St. Louis: Amerisearch, Inc. 2013.

Foster, Marshall and Mary-Elaine Swanson, *The American Covenant, The Untold Story*. USA: The Mayflower Institute, 1983.

Hall, Verna M. *The Christian History of the American Revolution*. San Francisco: The Foundation for Christian Education, 1976.

Hart, Benjamin. *Faith & Freedom: The Christian Roots of American Liberty*. Dallas: Lewis and Stanley, 1988.

Hyatt, Eddie. *Pilgrims and Patriots*. Grapevine, TX: Hyatt Press, 2016.

Hyatt, Susan. *In the Spirit We're Equal*. Dallas, TX: Hyatt Press, 1998.

Kidd, Thomas. *God of Liberty*. New York: Basic Books, 2010.

Marshall, Peter and David Manuel. *The Light and the Glory*. Grand Rapids: Fleming H. Revell, 1977.

Miller, Perry. *Errand Into the Wilderness*. Cambridge, MA: Harvard Univ. Press, 1956.

Noll, Mark A. *A History of Christianity in the United States and Canada*. Grand Rapids: Eerdmans, 1992.

Novak, William. *On Two Wings: Humble Faith and Common Sense at the American Founding*. San Francisco: Encounter Books, 2002.

Whitefield, George. *George Whitefield's Journals*. Carlisle, PA: Banner of Truth Trust, 1960.

About the Author

Dr. Eddie L. Hyatt is a seasoned minister of the Gospel with almost 50 years of ministerial experience as a pastor, Bible teacher and professor of theology. He holds the Doctor of Ministry degree from Regent University as well as both Master of Divinity and Master of Arts (historical/theological studies) degrees from Oral Roberts University. A prolific writer, he has authored numerous books, including *2000 Years of Charismatic Christianity*, which is used as a textbook in colleges and seminaries around the world. He has ministered in many nations over the years, but his current passion and commission is to call America back to her founding principles of freedom and Spiritual awakening. He is doing this through his writings and through the *1726 PROJECT*, a presentation which includes visual aids using Power Point, that is based on the contents of this book. Dr. Hyatt resides in Grapevine, TX with his wife, Dr. Susan Hyatt, where they are establishing the International Christian Women's Hall of Fame, Research and Ministry Center.

CONTACT INFORMATION

EMAIL: dreddiehyatt@gmail.com

WEBISITE: www.eddiehyatt.com

REGULAR MAIL: P. O. Box 3877, Grapevine, TX 76099

Dr. Hyatt's books are available at eddiehyatt.com and amazon.com. He is available to minister on various subjects, including *THE 1726 PROJECT* in your church, college, or community.

Resources by Dr Eddie L. Hyatt

Available on amazon.com in paperback & kindle
and at eddiehyatt.com

- Revival Fire: Discerning Between the True and the False
- Pilgrims and Patriots: The Radical Christian Roots of American Democracy and Freedom
- The Faith and Vision of Benjamin Franklin
- 5 Pillars of the American Republic
- The Great Prayer Awakening of 1857-58
- The Charismatic Luther
- George Whitefield
- Pursuing Power: How the Quest for Apostolic Authority and Control Has Divided and Damaged the Church
- Christmas is For Real" Evidence of the Virgin Birth
- 3 Keys to Answered Prayer
- Paul, Women and Church
- Who's the Boss? A Liberating Look at Ephesians 5:21-33

Classic Course Available from eddiehyatt.com